# THE PERFECT
# ENGLISH
# GRAMMAR
# WORKBOOK

Published by Callisto Publishing LLC C/O Sourcebooks LLC
P.O. Box 4410, Naperville, Illinois 60567-4410
(630) 961-3900
callistopublishing.com

Printed and bound in China.
WKT 20

# THE PERFECT ENGLISH GRAMMAR WORKBOOK

SIMPLE RULES AND QUIZZES TO
MASTER TODAY'S ENGLISH LANGUAGE

Lisa McLendon

CALLISTO PUBLISHING

# CONTENTS

COLOR KEY: ■ PRINCIPLES ■ COMPOSITION ■ STRUCTURE ■ WORDS ■ PUNCTUATION ■ USAGE AND STYLE

# INTRODUCTION

**A**s a linguist, an editor, and now a teacher—and a person who has loved words her whole life—I love taking language apart to see how it works, playing with it, and seeing what I can do with it. I spent years in graduate school studying Slavic languages and then more years in journalism; now I teach news editing at a university. I'm a total geek about grammar, and I'm not ashamed to admit it. But I'm definitely not a "grammar cop." I like the label *grammar cheerleader* a lot better, because grammar is a remarkable thing and a great tool for us, so we should give it a hearty *hoorah* from time to time.

Having worked in both academia and journalism, I approach language from several points of view: scholar, writer, and reader. I recognize that living languages change, so grammar advice from a century or even a couple of decades ago may not still be applicable today. But I also recognize that when you're trying to communicate clearly, with credibility and authority, there's a set of current standards you need to follow so that readers focus on what you're saying rather than how you're saying it. (Anyone who's ever made a typo on the Internet understands this.)

Teaching has given me new insight on grammar, though: Many people are apprehensive about writing and public speaking because they're not confident in their grammar skills. The fact that some guidebooks are complicated or snobby doesn't help. So I've made it a priority to "demystify" grammar: It's just a machine we all use already that occasionally has some tricky parts. Once you learn the tricky parts, you can use that machine like a pro.

A poster in my office reads, "Grammar is not a secret code." It is a code, sort of, but it's certainly not a secret. Grammar is for everyone, and everyone deserves to feel confident using it. The bigger point is that I wrote this book not to scold, but to support. It's for writers who want to learn more about language and how to use it according to current professional standards. Grammar doesn't have to be confusing and it doesn't have to be technical. It does take some practice—that's what this book offers—and with practice, you'll be perfect.

## How to Use This Book

This book is designed to quickly explain grammar rules and guidelines and to give you practice with them. The individual topics are sorted into seventeen chapters, which you don't have to do in order. In fact, you can skip around however you'd like. Search the index for something specific or browse the table of contents to see what you want to work on.

Each topic includes a brief explanation and a few examples, and most have a practice exercise for you to try. At the end of each chapter, there's a quiz that covers material from the whole chapter. The practice exercises and chapter quizzes are designed to make it fast and easy for you to check your work—all the answers are provided at the end of the book.

Grammar is a big, broad subject, and a book of this type can't cover it all. The topics in this book were chosen because they're the most common areas where people get confused or make mistakes. For an easy-to-use reference guide, the original *Perfect English Grammar* handbook is a great choice (this book was written as a companion to it). For deeper or more comprehensive questions, consult the "Further Reading" section at the end of this book.

A note about "Muphry's Law" (no, that's not a typo): This "law" states that any given piece of writing that attempts to offer language advice or correct mistakes in language will itself contain an error. Everything has been done to present you with a perfect book about perfect grammar, but any time human beings are involved, there's the possibility for error. I offer apologies in advance if a mistake slipped through.

## What Does This Book Mean by "Perfect English Grammar"?

You might have heard the saying "The perfect is the enemy of the good," meaning that if you fiddle with something too long to make it "perfect," you'll either never get it done or make a mess of it in the process. I like Vince Lombardi's take better: "We are going to relentlessly chase perfection, knowing full well we will not catch it . . . because in the process we will catch excellence."

Even if we hit only "excellent," "perfect" grammar is a good standard to aspire to—it opens doors for you academically and professionally, and it helps you communicate your information and ideas clearly. For the purposes of this book, I'm using a broader definition of "grammar": not just morphology and syntax, but all the rules and guidelines that govern language use, including spelling, punctuation, and usage. We have to understand the rules before we know when and why to break them (yes, we do break them sometimes). You won't want to blindly follow rules, but instead use them—or ignore them—to make your language clear and interesting.

The guidelines in this book reflect "standard American English"—that is, the English that's considered typical for an educated professional, the English you'll see in books and magazines, the English you'll hear on TV news and in the classroom. This doesn't mean that other ways of speaking and writing are bad or less valid—they aren't—it just means that if you're writing and speaking professionally, you'll probably want to follow this standard to reach a broad range of people and establish credibility with them.

One other twist: Because living languages change, "perfect grammar" is going to be a moving target over the course of your life. Once you have a solid grounding in the fundamental parts of the language, though, you'll be able to adjust easily and thoughtfully to changes as they come.

# 1.0

## WHY WE NEED GRAMMAR

PRINCIPLES

Language is a wonderful thing: It lets us communicate and inform, entertain and enlighten. Grammar is what holds it all together and helps it all make sense. Grammar grows and changes with language. It bends to accommodate poets and philosophers and physicists.

Grammar wasn't invented by a few lofty scholars to trip everyone else up. The original speakers of language created grammar, bit by bit, and the users of language, through the ages, have shaped and altered it to meet our needs (and sometimes our whims). Just as language is an integral part of our lives, grammar is, too.

But when grammar is ignored or confused, sentences come crashing down, paragraphs collapse, and meaning gets lost. Certainly sometimes people can figure out what you *meant*, even if it's not what you *said*, but other times your communication fails. People are confused. They misunderstand. They get distracted. You're not deliberately wasting breath or ink or bytes, but if you're not being clear, you might as well be. And that's why grammar is important: It makes language work. Remember that we control language—it doesn't control us. Use grammar as your tool to control language and make it work exactly how you want it to.

The good news is that you probably already know most of English grammar. If you're a native speaker of English, you've been using grammar ever since you learned to talk. We all use it, every time we speak or write, usually without even thinking about it. It's when we think about some parts of it that we start having doubts, which is why we have books like this one.

"Good enough" is fine for text messages and website comments and casual conversation. But if you're speaking or writing professionally, you want to give your teachers, bosses, clients, colleagues, and potential audiences better than "good enough." Don't all the people you communicate with deserve clear, clean, meaningful language? Perfect grammar won't give you something to say, but it will help you say it in the best way possible.

# 2.0
## GRAMMAR AND COMPOSITION

COMPOSITION

Although children pick up spoken language with ease, writing is a different skill, one that must be learned. And we're not just talking about handwriting or typing, but composing sentences, paragraphs, and narratives. The rules are different for writing. There are plenty of constructions you can use in speech that won't have the "grammar police" breaking down your door and carting you away, but when you write—if you want your ideas and information to be taken seriously—you'll want to avoid them.

This is a grammar workbook instead of a writing workbook, so we're not really going to focus on the details of writing essays, reports, or research papers, but here are a few tips and some practice exercises all about the elements of good composition.

## 2.1 General Writing Tips

Clean, clear grammar is the foundation for solid writing. No matter how good your ideas are or how relevant your facts might be, if they are presented in a confusing way, readers won't understand them. And if your content is presented through sloppy, scattered writing, readers won't take it seriously.

Writing is a craft. It takes work to get better, but with work you will get better. A good way to improve your writing is to read good examples of the kind of writing you're working on, so you can get a feel for how it's supposed to look.

Writing is a process. Most people don't just sit down and write something straight through. Instead, take it one step at a time: Think about your topic, gather information, organize your facts and your thoughts, write, revise, think some more, write some more, edit, and then format.

Different kinds of writing call for different styles. And "style" means both word choice and sentence structure, as well as the formatting, spelling, and punctuation choices in a document. For example, journalism is written in a more conversational style, and it usually follows Associated Press style. Academic writing is in a more formal style and often follows American Psychological Association (APA) or Modern Language Association (MLA) style.

## 2.2 Before You Begin

First, figure out what your goal is. That is, why are you writing? Are you writing to inform? Enlighten? Persuade? Entertain? Explore?

Then, figure out what your point is. Are you writing a news story about something that happened in your city? An analysis of imagery in a novel? A summary of research findings? An argument for or against a particular policy or viewpoint? Once you determine that, stay focused.

Next, figure out who your audience is. Are you writing for the general public? A scholarly audience? Children? Experts in a particular field? Your peers? People whose first language is not English? Your audience will determine how formal you want your writing to be, what sort of vocabulary you will use, and how complex your sentences and paragraphs will be.

Then, figure out what information you need to include and how much detail you need to go into. Gather your facts and analyze them. Always cite your sources!

Last, plan your composition. You don't have to do a traditional outline (though you may want to—lots of people find them helpful). Some people write each piece of information on an index card or a PowerPoint slide, to make it easy to put them in order and move things around. Some people jot down a brief list of topics in the order they want to write about them. There's no one right way to plan, but you should plan, so you know where you're going and how you're getting there.

## 2.3 Starting to Write

You don't have to start at the beginning, but you should at least start by writing a summary sentence. Think of it as the "elevator pitch" or the "headline" for what you're writing: It sums up what the point is and why your readers should care. If the rest of your plan doesn't match this summary, that's a red flag. It means you'll need to figure out whether to change your point or change your information.

The first paragraph is the entry into your composition. It needs to be clear and engaging, and it also needs to give the reader an idea of what's to come. You want to be specific about what your topic is, but don't get bogged down in details in that first paragraph.

Some people write down the details first, then go back and write the transitions and summaries. Others write everything in order. Find what works for you, but when you're ready to write, write. Write it all down—you'll revise it later. It's much easier to change something you've already written than to fill a blank page, so the sooner you get rid of the blank page, the better.

If you get stuck, talk it through. Find someone you know who's written for the audience you're writing for—or perhaps someone who is a member of that audience—and tell them about what you're writing. Explain why you're writing. Talk about the interesting things you've learned. Listen to any questions they might have.

## 2.4 Structure

Probably the most straightforward and best-known composition structure is introduction-body-conclusion. You can do this in five paragraphs (an intro, three paragraphs of body, a conclusion) or five pages or five chapters—give the readers an overview of your point, describe and detail the ideas that make your point, then wrap it all up with a summary. There's no rule that says the body needs to contain three supporting ideas instead of two or four or six, or that you can't add more sections, so you can adapt this structure to your material.

There's also no rule that says you have to stick with this structure at all. Creative work may follow a much looser structure, journalism a much tighter one. But no matter how you structure your composition, here are a few things to remember:

- **Start with something good:** You want to catch and hold the reader's attention. Be clear about what your point is and be as interesting as you can be.

- **Stay focused on the point:** Don't wander off on a tangent that doesn't support or relate to your point. But, you might say, that tangent is really interesting! If you find yourself saying that, think about this: If it's that interesting, why isn't it your main point? Maybe you need to revisit your plan (which is fine—writers do it all the time).
- **Support your point with examples and facts.** Even if you are writing an opinion, having data or specific examples to back it up makes your argument stronger. And always credit your sources.
- **Flow from one idea into the next,** both logically and through use of transitions. You want the reader to stay with you and understand the progression of ideas and information.

## 2.5 Transitions

When you're linking ideas together, transitions are what help you lead the reader from one idea to the next. They make your writing flow smoothly and allow the reader to follow your train of thought.

Transition words or phrases can begin a sentence to tie that idea to the previous idea. Sometimes you might need a whole sentence or even a whole (brief) paragraph to transition between ideas. The important thing is not to swerve from one idea to the next without a transition.

Transitions usually fall into one of these categories:

- **Addition or similarity:** moreover, likewise, also, in addition, in the same way, etc.
- **Contrast or opposition:** conversely, although, but, despite, nevertheless, etc.
- **Examples or emphasis:** in fact, especially, in particular, for instance, etc.
- **Results or effects:** therefore, consequently, thus, as a result, etc.
- **Time or sequence:** first, second, third, etc.; before, after, meanwhile, etc.
- **Conclusion or summary:** finally, in conclusion, in summary, all in all, etc.

This is by no means an exhaustive list, but it gives you an idea of what sorts of words and phrases work as transitions.

**PRACTICE EXERCISE 2.5**

# TRANSITIONS

Think about the transition categories and then choose the correct answer.

1. Which of these transitions sets up a contrast?
   a. however
   b. likewise
   c. second

2. Which of these transitions sets up an example?
   a. additionally
   b. specifically
   c. despite

3. Which of these transitions sets up an addition?
   a. furthermore
   b. although
   c. due to

4. Which of these transitions sets up a result?
   a. also
   b. indeed
   c. in effect

5. Which of these transitions sets up a conclusion?
   a. first
   b. to sum up
   c. on the other hand

*(continued)*

## 2.6 Common Pitfalls

No matter what you're writing, or what structure you're following, you want to be aware of common writing pitfalls. We rarely say *never* in language, but here are a few things it's usually better to avoid:

- **Wordiness:** Why use five words when one would do? Excess verbiage doesn't make you sound smart, it just makes your writing a slog to read. Too many words and not enough substance will distract or bore readers, neither of which you want.

- **Clichés:** If something's a cliché, it's so well known that it's lost its "oomph." You want your writing to be fresh and engaging, not tired and dull. This doesn't mean to never use clichés, but to stop when you write one to see whether you could be more vivid, more specific, or more interesting. If something is "like shooting fish in a barrel" or "as easy as pie," how much does that tell the reader? Could you convey the same information in a more specific way, such as, "it takes only 10 minutes"?

- **Too much detail:** Find the example, statistic, or fact that best illustrates your point and leave it at that. No need to hit readers over the head with a load of repetitive support.

- **Not enough detail:** You do, however, need to support your point. Don't expect readers to simply take your word for it—back up your ideas with concrete information.

- **No single, overarching theme:** This shows up as two problems. One is having no clear point at all, which leaves a reader confused or frustrated. The other is having too many competing points, which means the reader can't figure out what to focus on.

---

**PRACTICE EXERCISE 2.6**

## COMMON PITFALLS

Match each wordy phrase with its more concise alternative.

| | | |
|---|---|---|
| 1. | due to the fact that | yellow |
| 2. | on a regular basis | because |
| 3. | has the ability to | decided |
| 4. | yellow in color | can |
| 5. | came to the decision that | regularly |

**KEY FOR PRACTICE EXERCISE 2.6**
1. because
2. regularly
3. can
4. yellow
5. decided

## 2.7 Editing

Once you're done writing, you're not finished yet—you still need to edit. Editing is far more than running spell-check (you *do* run spell-check, right?). It involves details such as making sure you've used words correctly, spelled names right, and punctuated everything properly, as well as bigger issues such as making sure your writing flows, your ideas are supported, and your numbers add up.

It's best to have another person edit your work, because they aren't familiar with your point and their fresh eyes will spot places where you've jumped too far ahead without connection, you haven't explained something clearly enough, or you've made typos your own tired eyes can no longer notice.

If you need to edit your own work, you can do a few things to make it more successful:

- **Take a break:** During the writing process, we become so engrossed with writing that we can't see our own mistakes. After clearing your head, you can take a fresh look.
- **Read it out loud:** This makes sentences that are awkward, overwrought, or poorly punctuated jump out at you.
- **Read it backward or change the type style when proofreading:** This helps you focus on the words from a perspective different from the one you used for writing.
- **Make a list of things you know you always mess up:** For example, if you know you have a habit of typing "form" when you mean "from"—I'm really bad about that—then do a search for every instance of "form," so you can find and fix the ones where you really meant "from."

Why is it important to edit? It all comes down to presenting a polished piece of writing to your readers. It helps your writing be taken seriously in a way that error-riddled, disorganized writing won't be. Editing your work says to readers that you value the time and attention they're giving you, and that you respect them enough to give them writing that is as close to perfect as it can be.

# 3.0

# PARTS OF
# SPEECH

## STRUCTURE

The parts of speech are the categories to which all words belong. They let us classify what a word does in a sentence. Unlike many other languages, English lets some words shift from one part of speech to another without any changes to them. If you've heard about people "verbing" nouns, that's what this is—except we've also "adverbed" prepositions, "nouned" verbs, and "adjectived" nouns. Sometimes people do it on purpose; other times, a word broadens its scope naturally, falling into several categories. As a result, thousands of English words fall into more than one part of speech, and what category it is depends on what role it has in a particular sentence.

We'll briefly define the parts of speech here, then explain each one in more detail in later chapters.

- **Verbs** indicate an action or a state of being. Examples of verbs: walk, think, seem, assemble, become. (See chapter 6.)
- **Nouns** are people, places, things, ideas, or concepts. Examples of nouns: Elvis, studio, guitar, talent, fame. (See chapter 8.)
- **Determiners** go with a noun or noun phrase to shape its meaning. Examples of determiners: the, a/an, my, many, some, that. (See chapter 7.)
- **Pronouns** stand in for a noun or noun phrase, so you don't have to keep repeating it. Examples of pronouns: you, me, her, they, who, these. (See chapter 10.)
- **Adjectives** describe a noun, usually answering the question "what kind?" or "which one?" Examples of adjectives: green, tall, friendly, difficult. (See chapter 11.)
- **Adverbs** describe a verb, adjective, or other adverb, usually answering the question "where?" "when" "how?" or "why?" Examples of adverbs: quietly, totally, very, too. (See chapter 12.)

- **Prepositions** tie nouns to other information in the sentence. A prepositional phrase can work as an adjective, describing a noun; or as an adverb, describing a verb, adjective, or other adverb. Examples of prepositions: in, on, by, over, after. (See chapter 13.)
- **Conjunctions** join words, phrases, or clauses in a sentence. Examples of conjunctions: and, but, either . . . or, whenever. (See chapter 14.)
- **Interjections** are outbursts that indicate strong emotion. Examples of interjections: Ouch! Awesome! Oh, no! and many other reactions replaceable by emoji. (See chapter 15.)

## QUIZ FOR CHAPTER 3: PARTS OF SPEECH

For questions 1–10, match the word with its part of speech.

| | | |
|---|---|---|
| 1. | blue | noun |
| 2. | the | adjective |
| 3. | Yikes! | adverb |
| 4. | bus | conjunction |
| 5. | perform | interjection |
| 6. | quickly | preposition |
| 7. | but | pronoun |
| 8. | in | noun |
| 9. | we | determiner |
| 10. | freedom | verb |

For questions 11–15, refer to the following sentence:

**Once the scientists returned from Alaska, they calculated their climatic data.**

11.   Write down the noun(s), but not the pronouns, in the sentence:

_____

12.   Write down the verb(s) in the sentence:

_____

13.   Write down the adjective(s) in the sentence:

_____

14.    Write down the conjunction(s) in the sentence:

_____

15.    Write down the preposition(s) in the sentence:

_____

For questions 16–20, refer to the following sentence:

**Hey, you can't go into the reactor—the radiation is too dangerous.**

16.    Write down the pronoun(s), but not the nouns, in the sentence:

17.    Write down the verb(s) in the sentence:

18.    Write down the adverb(s) in the sentence:

19.    Write down the interjections(s) in the sentence:

20.    Write down the determiner(s) in the sentence:

_____

*Answers can be found on page 196.*

# 4.0
## SPELLING AND STYLE

**STRUCTURE**

As you know by this point in your life, English spelling is, to put it bluntly, a hot mess. Few words are spelled as they sound, and we have a jumble of silent letters, varying vowels, and words that sound the same but aren't spelled the same—not to mention the words that are spelled the same but don't sound the same! Then there are things like numbers that can be rendered using either letters or digits.

Some of these choices aren't between a "right" way and a "wrong" way but are arbitrary preferences that vary depending on what you're writing and, thus, what style guide you're following. Some commonly used style guides are the *MLA Handbook*, *The Chicago Manual of Style*, and *The Associated Press Stylebook*.

This chapter will cover some of the basic principles of spelling and style and give you tips and practice with common trouble spots.

## 4.1 How to Improve Your Spelling

One-word answer: *Read.* Read a variety of good writing: fiction, nonfiction, poetry, essays, criticism, journalism. Push yourself to read deeper and more complex texts. The more you read, the more words you encounter and the more familiar you become with them. When a word becomes familiar, it will look right to you, and you won't even have to think about spelling it.

When you come across a word you don't know, write it down. Research has shown that the physical act of writing helps people remember better. Then look up the word to see what it means in context, plus what else it can mean. (Merriam-Webster, Oxford, and Dictionary.com all offer free apps for iOS and Android, so you can look up words on your phone wherever you are.) You may need to look up a word a few times, especially if a lot of time passes between when you first see it and when you reencounter it. Look at any related words as well, such as the verb form of a noun or the noun form of an adjective. See how those words are put together—for instance, how endings are attached or how certain consonants change.

# HOW TO IMPROVE YOUR SPELLING

Look up the underlined word in the sentence below, even if you already know it, in your favorite dictionary. Then answer the questions below.

**Because lizards are not <u>homeothermic</u>, they have a narrower range of habitats than birds.**

1. What is the definition of the word?

2. What is the part of speech of the word?

3. How is the word pronounced?

4. Are there any alternative spellings of the word?

5. What other forms of the word are given in the dictionary, and what parts of speech are they? (You may need to look at the entries above and below the word itself.)

**KEY FOR PRACTICE EXERCISE 4.1**

1. warm-blooded, or maintaining a constant body temperature that is not dependent on the environmental temperature

2. adjective

3. HO-mee-oh-THUR-mik

4. homoiothermic

5. homeotherm (noun), homeothermy (noun), homeothermism (noun), homeothermal (adjective)

## 4.2 Common Spelling Errors

With autocorrect and spell-check, it's easier than ever to not worry about spelling. However, you still need to pay attention, because computers can't read our minds (yet), so they may suggest a word that looks like what you've typed but isn't what you meant.

There are three major trouble spots:

- Words that aren't the words you want but are still words, such as solider when you meant soldier or loose when you meant lose.
- British spellings when you're writing for a US audience, such as endeavour for endeavor or centre for center. These aren't wrong, but because they aren't the typical American spellings, they may distract your readers. (Many spell-checkers flag British variants.)
- Homophones, which are words that sound the same but have different spellings and meanings, such as affect and effect or principle and principal.

When in doubt, look it up.

# COMMON SPELLING ERRORS

Choose the best answer. Look up the words if you need to—or just for fun!

1. When you get to the stadium, park in the A section, **than / then** meet us at the south entrance.

2. Melinda was born in a hardware store a half hour after her mother went into **labor / labour**.

3. How many times did you get sent to the **principle's / principal's** office in grade school?

4. We are **definitely / defiantly** coming to the cookout, so save us some potato salad!

5. Their youngest daughter has been **accepted / excepted** into a zookeeper-training program.

**PRACTICE EXERCISE 4.2**

1. then
2. labor
3. principal's
4. definitely
5. accepted

## 4.3 Affixes and Common Spelling Rules

Affixes are things that get added to words. **Prefixes**—such as *pre-* and *post-* and *trans-,* among many others—get tacked on to the beginning. **Suffixes**—such as *-tion* and *-ing* and *-ment*—latch on to the end. **Infixes**, which we don't use much in English except in slang or swearing, get dropped into the middle, as in *fan-freaking-tastic.* **Inflected endings** are suffixes on nouns and verbs that indicate number or tense (for more on this, see chapter 6: Verbs and chapter 8: Nouns).

With suffixes in particular, English has a few spelling rules that work pretty consistently:

- For words that end in -e, drop the -e when you add a suffix starting in a vowel, but leave the -e when the suffix starts with a consonant: dance, dancing, dancer. Exceptions are words that end -ee, -oe and -ye: hoe, hoeing; eye, eyeing.
- For words that end in -y, change the -y to an -i before a suffix, unless the suffix starts with i: rally, rallied, rallying; early, earlier.
- For one-syllable, one-vowel words that end in one consonant, we usually double the last consonant when adding a suffix: set, setting, setter; whir, whirring, whirred.

(And forget *"i* before *e* except after *c"*—that "rule" has so many exceptions that it's practically useless.)

# COMMON SPELLING RULES

Using the underlined word in the first sentence, fill in the correct form in the blank in the second sentence.

1.  Chop, don't <u>mince</u>, the onion. But take care when _____ the garlic so the pieces are uniform.

2.  Their dog is really <u>hairy</u>. I don't think I've ever seen a _____ dog than theirs.

3.  Perez is next up to <u>bat</u>. He is _____ over .300 this month.

4.  Did that writer just <u>dangle</u> a participle? _____ participles are a grammar no-no. (See page 92 for more about participles.)

5.  We have an <u>ally</u> in the marketing department, but we need even more _____ in R&D.

**KEY FOR PRACTICE EXERCISE 4.3**

1.  mincing
2.  hairier
3.  batting
4.  dangling
5.  allies

## 4.4 Contractions

Contractions are formed when two words combine into one and lose a letter (or several) in the process. Where the letters drop out, we put in an apostrophe.

Contractions most commonly occur with **noun + *is, will***, with **pronoun + *is, are, are, will, has, have, had,*** and with **verb + *not***. For example, "Rob is eating becomes Rob's eating, we are becomes we're, did not becomes didn't, could have becomes could've, and so on. Let's is used for let us and is fine for suggestions and requests. Y'all is the contraction of you all, which is common in speech but best avoided in formal writing. Notice that the apostrophes go where the missing letters were.

There's nothing wrong with using contractions in writing: They are grammatical and a perfectly legitimate part of English. In fact, deliberately avoiding contractions in writing makes it sound stuffy and stilted. That said, don't overuse contractions, and be mindful of what your audience expects.

**PRACTICE EXERCISE 4.4**

## CONTRACTIONS

Match each contraction with the phrase it's short for.

| | | |
|---|---|---|
| 1. | you're | they are |
| 2. | you've | you are |
| 3. | they're | you have |
| 4. | they'd | should have |
| 5. | should've | they had |

*(continued)*

35

*(continued)*

**KEY FOR PRACTICE EXERCISE 4.4**

1. you are
2. you have
3. they are
4. they had
5. should have

## 4.5 Possessive Pitfalls

Speaking of apostrophes, we use them for things other than contractions. An apostrophe plus an *s* (*'s*) is what we use to mark possessive nouns: *Mom's rosebushes, my sister's new baby.* For plural possessives, the *s* comes first, then the apostrophe (*s'*): *the candidates' debate, the Millers' house.* When it comes to possessives for singular nouns ending in *s*, style guides vary (that is, there's more than one right way to do it), but the more common way is to go ahead and add apostrophe + *s*: *Ross's friends, the bus's windshield.* Ditto for abbreviations: *the TV's features, the FBI's Most Wanted.*

With nouns, apostrophes are *not* used to make simple plurals, no matter how many grocery store signs you've seen to the contrary. So: *We bought bananas. Bananas were on sale.* No apostrophe. But once you make a noun possessive, here comes the apostrophe: *That banana's stem is broken. These bananas' color is a little too green.* One exception in many style guides is single letters: *She has all A's this term.*

You might think that, logically, we'd use apostrophes to mark possessive pronouns as well as possessive nouns, but we don't: you-your-yours, it-its, we-our-ours, etc. Not an apostrophe in sight. Here's the trick for pronouns: When you see an apostrophe, say the contraction as two words. If it makes sense, keep the apostrophe; if it doesn't, ditch the apostrophe. For example: Can we take **you're** car to the concert? Say *you're* as two words: Can we take **you are** car to the concert? That doesn't make sense, so use *your* instead of *you're*.

# POSSESSIVE PITFALLS

Use the word above each sentence to fill in a plural and/or a possessive that fits the sentence's meaning.

1. **Ford**

   That dealer sells new and used _____. The F-150 is _____ best-selling pickup.

2. **employee**

   The store has 12 full-time _____. The _____ uniforms are green and yellow.

3. **they**

   _____ house is being painted this week.

4. **you**

   Just because all _____ friends are doing it doesn't mean you should, too.

5. **band**

   Our marching _____ performance was good enough to win first place. Nearly a hundred other _____ were in the competition.

**KEY FOR PRACTICE EXERCISE 4.5**

1. Fords, Ford's
2. employees; employees'
3. Their
4. your
5. band's; bands

## 4.6 Dates and Times

The reason dates and times can be confusing is that we can render them multiple ways. Use only numbers or spell out months? The whole year or the last two digits? Abbreviate months and days of the week? How? Is it a.m. or A.M. and does it even need the periods? This is where a style guide comes in handy because it answers all these questions for you. That doesn't mean other ways are wrong, but it's good to stick to a consistent way of styling dates and times within a document.

That said, here are a few things the style guides generally agree on:

- US dates are written as "month, day, year": January 31, 1997. Much of the rest of the world writes "day, month, year": 31 January 1997. Remember this when you see a date such as 11/5/16: In the United States, that's November 5, 2016; elsewhere, it's probably May 11, 2016.

- The day is always written with numerals, not spelled out: Graduation is June 2 (not "June second"). If you're talking only about the day, use the ordinal but still write it with numerals: I'm busy on the 12th, but I can meet on the 13th.

- If you have a full date within a sentence, the year is set off by commas: The D-Day assault on June 6, 1944, was led by General Dwight Eisenhower. Don't forget the comma after the year.

- How and when to abbreviate months and days of the week varies, but if the month or day is the only time element given, spell it out: We're meeting Tuesday. His birthday is in February.

- When talking about a decade, the apostrophe is placed where the missing numbers are: I love the '80s (not "the 80's"; also, make sure the apostrophe faces the proper direction—some word processors automatically think it's a single quote and turn it the wrong way).

- When talking about a time of day, if you specify a.m. or p.m., you don't need "in the morning" or "in the evening," and vice versa—it's redundant to double up.

- Use o'clock only on the hour: the 6 o'clock news. Specify morning or evening if it's unclear from the context.

- Midnight and noon are usually clearer than 12 a.m. and 12 p.m., but midnight can sometimes be ambiguous, so clarify if needed: Friday night just before midnight, Saturday morning just after midnight. If you use noon or midnight, you don't also need to say 12.

- If you use approximations such as around, use a rounded-off time, not a specific time: The 911 call came in shortly after 10 p.m. (not "shortly after 10:08 p.m."—if you can be that specific, then don't fudge it).

- Biweekly, bimonthly, and biannual are, at this point, hopelessly muddled. Specify twice a week/month/year or every two weeks/months/years to be clear.

# DATES AND TIMES

Choose the best answer. Assume US English.

1. The committee chairs meet every _____ to plan the agenda.
   a. Wed.
   b. Wednesday

2. _____ is a date that will live in infamy.
   a. December 7, 1941,
   b. December 7, 1941
   c. 7 December 1941

3. He works nights, so don't call before _____ .
   a. 9 a.m. in the morning
   b. 9 a.m.
   c. 9 o'clock

4. Growing up in the _____, she had fewer career options than women today do.
   a. 50s
   b. 50's
   c. '50s

5. When they heard a knock at the door _____, they wondered who it could be.
   a. around 4 a.m.
   b. around 3:56 a.m.

**KEY FOR PRACTICE EXERCISE 4.6**

1. b
2. a
3. b
4. c
5. a

## 4.7 Numbers

As with dates and times, a style guide is a great resource for how to render numbers, and, as with dates and times, the important thing is to be consistent throughout a document. Here are a few things the style guides generally agree on:

- Spell out numbers zero to nine, and spell out any number at the beginning of a sentence (this may require rewording a sentence that starts with a big number).
- For numbers of four or more digits, put a comma every third number counting from the right: 5,280; 22,000; 3,495,122.
- Fractions are more commonly used in casual language, such as recipes or approximations, otherwise, spell it out (about half the people there).
- Decimals are used for more precise figures. For a number less than zero, add a zero before the decimal point: 0.67, 0.005.
- For dollar amounts, use either the dollar sign or the word dollars, but not both. If you use the dollar sign, use numerals for the amount: $5, five dollars. Ditto for cents, if anyone still uses the cents sign. And remember that 25 cents is $0.25, not 0.25 cents—it's one-quarter, or 0.25, of a dollar, not a penny.
- The letters K (for thousands), M (for millions), and B (for billions) are generally used only in headlines and specialized publications.
- For percentages, use either the percent sign or the word percent, but not both. Use numerals for the percentage in either case: a 7 percent solution, the interest rate is 3.25%.

You may run across the terms *cardinal* and *ordinal* for numbers. **Cardinal** numbers are the counting numbers: one, two, three, etc. **Ordinal** numbers are the sequence numbers (that is, they put things in order): first, second, third, etc. The same rules for spelling them out or using numerals apply to both types.

Expressions such as *a couple of, a few, several, some, a number of, a bunch of, many,* and *a lot of* are common in casual language and are used when a precise quantity is either unknown or irrelevant. Use a plural verb with them.

It's okay to pronounce a zero as *oh* when it's clear that you're talking about numbers, such as in phone numbers (867-5309 as *eight-six-seven-five-three-oh-nine*) and years (1908 as *nineteen-oh-eight*).

---

**PRACTICE EXERCISE 4.7**

## NUMBERS

Choose the best answer.

1. Leadville, Colorado, is the highest city in the United States, with an elevation of _____ feet.
   a. 10,152
   b. 101,52
   c. 10152

2. The average cost of a new car in the United States in 2015 was _____.
   a. $33,560 dollars
   b. $33,560
   c. 33K dollars

3. The Krakowskis have _____ people in their family and _____ dogs.
   a. 5, 6
   b. 5, six
   c. five, six

4. Storms and 95-degree temperatures didn't keep _____ fans from the outdoor music festival.

   a. fifty thousand

   b. 50,000

   c. 50K

5. In the mid-1980s, mortgage rates were around _____.

   a. twelve %

   b. twelve percent

   c. 12 percent

**KEY FOR PRACTICE EXERCISE 4.7**

1. a

2. b

3. c

4. b

5. c

## QUIZ FOR CHAPTER 4: SPELLING AND STYLE

For questions 1–4, turn the underlined phrase into a contraction.

1.  I prefer to visit Paris when <u>it is</u> not hot and crowded. _____

2.  While <u>you are</u> at the store, can you get some milk?_____

3.  Paul <u>should have</u> known better with a girl like her. _____

4.  We <u>did not</u> see a thing. _____

For questions 5–8, circle the best answer. Look up the words if necessary.

5.  One of the medication's side **affects / effects** was hallucinations.

6.  The police found shell casings that matched the **caliber / calibre** of the fatal bullet.

7.  Because Rachel's a book blogger, she gets a sneak **peak / peek / pique** at new releases.

8.  The development team has free **rein / reign** on the new project—and a huge budget.

For questions 9–12, fill in the correct form of the given word.

9.  **scary**
The sequel was much _____ than the first movie.

10.  **puddle**
Water was _____ on the floor underneath the leak in the roof.

11.  **rat**
The gangster couldn't believe his buddies _____ him out to the Feds.

12.  **army**
The video game involves warring _____ of monsters.

For questions 13–16, use the given word to fill in a plural and/or a possessive that fits the sentence's meaning.

13. **it**

The spectators cheered when the monster truck was knocked clean off

_____ chassis.

14. **kitten**

At the Humane Society, there are dozens of _____ waiting to be adopted.

15. **PBS**

Sherlock is one of _____ most popular shows.

16. **you**

Why haven't you finished _____ homework yet?

For questions 17–24, circle the best answer.

17. They stood in line for the **midnight / 12 a.m. / 12 midnight** movie.

18. Marcy's Aunt Agnes was born on **November 19, 1911, / November 19, 1911** in Chicago.

19. Because of Wiley's success on the Acme account, he got a **$3K / $3,000 / $3,000 dollar** bonus.

20. Millie was so excited the day she reached **10K / 100,00 / 10,000** followers on Twitter.

21. All four of the Wongs' children have **December / Dec**. birthdays.

22. When you go to the boss's house for dinner, mind **you're p's and q's / your p's and q's / your ps and qs**.

23. **First / 1st / 1th**, you need to turn on the machine.

24. The music scene in the late **60's / 60s / '60s** was groovy, man.

---

*Answers can be found on page 196–197.*

# 5.0

## SENTENCE STRUCTURE

STRUCTURE

We covered parts of speech in chapter 3 and word-level issues of spelling and style in chapter 4. In this chapter, we'll move on to how to put sentences together.

## 5.1 Subjects and Predicates

The subject of a sentence is a noun or pronoun that does the action or is something. The subject almost always comes before the verb, but it may not be at the very beginning of a sentence, and there may be other words between the subject and the verb. The predicate is simply what finishes the sentence. It's the verb, usually with a direct object (see section 5.3) or a subject complement (see section 5.7).

It's easy to see the division in a simple sentence:

*Harold built a surveillance machine.*

*Harold* is the subject: He's doing something. *Built a surveillance machine* is the predicate: It's what happened.

subject | predicate
*Harold | built a surveillance machine.*

But when we add more words, you may need to hunt a little for the subject and predicate:

*After the exam, Alyssa, who hadn't studied, knew she had done well.*

*After the exam* starts the sentence but isn't doing or being anything, so it is not the subject. *Alyssa* is a noun, and she's doing something, so there's your subject. *Who hadn't studied* is something that happened (see section 5.4: Clauses), but it's not the main thing that happened. *Knew she had done well* is the main thing that happened, so there's your predicate.

subject | predicate
*After the exam, Alyssa, who hadn't studied, | knew she had done well.*

With questions, the word order is a little different because we put the subject between an auxiliary verb (see section 6.1) and the main verb:

*Did you find anything?*

The pronoun *you* is the subject. *Did find anything* is the predicate.

---

## SUBJECTS AND PREDICATES

In each sentence, draw a line right before the predicate.

1. Sir Fluffypants caught three mice this morning.

2. He was very proud of himself.

3. But because of the carnage, an awful mess on the carpet needed to be cleaned up.

4. We really shouldn't let him out before breakfast.

5. Now, after all his activity, he's asleep on the couch.

### KEY FOR PRACTICE EXERCISE 5.1

1. Sir Fluffypants | caught three mice this morning.
2. He | was very proud of himself.
3. But because of the carnage, an awful mess on the carpet | needed to be cleaned up.
4. We | really shouldn't let him out before breakfast.
5. Now, after all his activity, he |'s asleep on the couch. (The 's in the contraction is the main verb, *is*.)

## 5.2 Subject-Verb Agreement

*Agreement* in a grammatical sense means that elements of a sentence have to match up with each other. Subjects and verbs are two elements that have to agree in number (see section 6.3)—that is, a singular subject goes with a singular verb and a plural subject goes with a plural verb.

This is usually pretty straightforward, but—at this point you should not be surprised—there are some trouble spots:

Compound subjects (joined with *and*) are plural.

*<u>Cameron and Sloane</u> were laughing as they watched Ferris jump onto a float and sing.*

Intervening phrases or clauses can throw you off, but remember: Even if there's a plural noun at the end of a phrase or clause, it's not the subject, so it doesn't affect the verb. Use only the subject to decide which verb you need.

*The <u>CEO</u>, accompanied by three board members, <u>was</u> seated at the head table.*

Indefinite pronouns—everyone, anyone, someone, each—take a singular verb:

*<u>Everybody knows</u> that Angelo's has the best pizza.*

With compound subjects joined by *either . . . or* or *neither . . . nor* (see section 14.2), the verb agrees with the closest subject:

*Neither the workers nor <u>the supervisor wants</u> to compromise.*

*Neither the supervisor nor <u>the workers want</u> to compromise.*

# SUBJECT-VERB AGREEMENT

In each sentence, circle the correct verb.

1. The dog, along with her owners, **is / are** playing in the park.

2. Each team **has / have** been practicing all week for Sunday's game.

3. Either the coach or the assistants **has/ have** to decide the starting lineup.

4. Brendan's radio show and Laura's podcast **feature / features** a lot of local music.

5. Our mayor, just like most other politicians, never **know / knows** when to keep quiet.

**KEY FOR PRACTICE EXERCISE 5.2**

1. is (*dog* is singular)
2. has
3. have (*assistants* is the closest subject)
4. feature
5. knows (*mayor* is singular)

## 5.3 Objects

A **direct object** follows an action verb and answers the question "Whom?" or "What?" A direct object is a noun or a pronoun, or it can be a whole clause. Not all action verbs require direct objects, but most can take them.

*The children at the party ate cake.*
*Cake* is what they ate, the direct object.

*Then they played a game.*
*Game* is what they played, the direct object.

An **indirect object** comes between the action verb and the direct object and answers the question "To whom or what?" or "For whom or what?" Indirect objects are recipients and occur with verbs that have the sense of giving, showing, or telling. An indirect object is always a noun or pronoun and almost never appears by itself without a direct object.

*The guests brought the birthday girl presents.*
*Presents* is what they brought, the direct object, and *the birthday girl* is who received them, the indirect object.

*Her mother showed us photos of the party later.*
*Photos* are what she showed, the direct object, and *us* is who saw them, the indirect object.

The **object of a preposition** is a noun or pronoun, or sometimes a whole clause, that follows a preposition to complete a prepositional phrase (see section 5.6).

*The party was held in Watson Park.*
*Watson Park* is the object of the preposition *in*.

*The partygoers' parents sat under a big oak tree.*
*Tree* is the object of the preposition *under*.

# OBJECTS

In each sentence, identify the function of the underlined word.

1. Peter sent his <u>mother</u> flowers for her birthday.

   **direct object**     **indirect object**     **object of a preposition**

2. Joel will be going home after <u>dinner</u>.

   **direct object**     **indirect object**     **object of a preposition**

3. Will you return the <u>gift</u> to the address on the envelope?

   **direct object**     **indirect object**     **object of a preposition**

4. Kelly sent her <u>classmates</u> an email about the group project.

   **direct object**     **indirect object**     **object of a preposition**

5. I found your car keys in the <u>bathroom</u>—they must have fallen out of your pocket.

   **direct object**     **indirect object**     **object of a preposition**

**KEY FOR PRACTICE EXERCISE 5.3**

1. indirect object
2. object of a preposition
3. direct object
4. indirect object
5. object of a preposition

## 5.4 Clauses

A clause is a group of words that has a subject and a predicate (see section 5.1). Sounds like a sentence, right? But clauses can be **independent** or **dependent**. Independent clauses are complete sentences—they can stand on their own. But dependent clauses, also called **subordinate clauses**, are not complete sentences—they have to be part of a larger sentence.

> *We were late.*
> Independent clause, complete sentence

> *Because we were late,*
> Dependent clause, not a complete sentence—you're expecting some additional information to follow when you encounter a clause like this.

The easiest way to tell whether you have a dependent clause is to say it out loud. If you find yourself wondering "Aaaaaand?" as if there should be more to the sentence, then you probably have a dependent clause. Or you can look for **subordinators**, which we'll get to in the next section.

Two independent clauses can be joined with a coordinating conjunction such as "and" or "but" (see section 14.1) to create a **compound sentence**, in which neither clause is subordinate. When there's a subordinate clause attached to the main clause, you get a **complex sentence**.

> Compound sentence: *He cooks and we clean up.* (Two independent clauses.)

> Complex sentence: *After he cooks, we clean up.* (Dependent clause plus independent clause.)

## CLAUSES

Identify the type of clause.

1. Because she's your friend
   **independent**    **dependent**

2. When I find myself overwhelmed with work
   **independent**    **dependent**

3. Yesterday, Sam and Shana finished their project
   **independent**    **dependent**

4. She came in covered with mud
   **independent**    **dependent**

5. Though the news was late because of the football game
   **independent**    **dependent**

### KEY FOR PRACTICE EXERCISE 5.4

1. dependent
2. dependent
3. independent
4. independent
5. dependent

## 5.5 Subordinators

**Subordinators** are words that link a clause to another clause, making it a dependent, or subordinate, clause (see previous section). Subordinators fall into two main categories: relative pronouns (see section 10.6) and subordinating conjunctions (see section 14.3).

The **relative pronouns** are *who, whom, which, that* and their indefinite forms *whoever, whomever, whichever*. Relative clauses introduce more information about a noun. The relative pronoun can serve as the subject or an object in the clause.

> *Luke, who grew up on Tatooine, never thought he'd be back.*
> *Who grew up on Tatooine* is the subordinate clause, with *who* as the subject and *grew up* as the verb.

> *The Death Star plans, which the Bothan spies stole, were used to plot the attack. Which the Bothan spies stole* is the subordinate clause, with *which* as the direct object of the verb *stole*.

**Subordinating conjunctions** are conjunctions such as *until, unless, if, how, wherever, because, after,* and *although,* among others. They often indicate a time frame or a consequence.

> *Once we finished our essays, we could enjoy the beautiful day.*
> "Once" is the subordinating conjunction, and *we finished our essays* becomes a subordinate clause once *once* introduces it.

**PRACTICE EXERCISE 5.5**

## SUBORDINATORS

Identify the subordinator in each sentence.

1.  If there's something wrong with your refrigerator, Billy Sue can fix it.    _____

2.  We were worried because she looked as if she'd seen a ghost.
    _____

3.  These crazy people who say they "bust ghosts" are a menace!
    _____

4.  But the ghost that haunted the library is gone.
    _____

5.  Egon knows what to do whenever there's a paranormal problem.
    _____

**KEY FOR PRACTICE EXERCISE 5.5**

1.  If
2.  because
3.  who
4.  that
5.  whenever

## 5.6 Phrases

A phrase is a group of words that work as a single unit of meaning but not as a complete sentence. It might have a subject or predicate, but it doesn't have both.

- **Prepositional phrases** modify something in the sentence. They usually work like adjectives (answering "What kind?" or "Which one?") or adverbs (answering "Where?" "When?" "How?" or "Why?"). They can occur with other objects or with complements, or simply with a subject and verb. *In their house, off the charts*, and *despite the rain* are examples of prepositional phrases.

- **Noun phrases** consist of a noun plus any determiners (see chapter 7), adjectives (see chapter 11), and other things that modify the noun, such as prepositional and participial phrases. The whole thing works like one big stuck-together noun unit—remember this for agreement purposes. *This old house, her brother in Amsterdam*, and *that doggie in the window* are examples of noun phrases.

- **Verb phrases** consist of a verb (see chapter 6) and any adverbs and objects that go with it. Roger <u>*has always been interested in clothes*</u>. *Has been* is the main verb, *always* is an adverb, and interested in clothes is the subject complement (see next section).

- **Infinitive phrases** use the infinitive form of the verb (see section 6.11) and usually function like a noun in a sentence. *Roger prefers <u>to wear suits and hats</u>. To wear* is the infinitive; the phrase functions as the direct object of *prefer*.

- **Participial phrases** use the participle form of the verb (see section 6.11) and usually function like an adjective in a sentence: <u>*Wearing a seersucker suit and straw hat*</u>, *Roger stuck out among his fellow students. Wearing* is the participle that heads up the phrase, which modifies *Roger*.

## PHRASES

In each sentence, identify the type of phrase that is underlined.

1.  <u>Trudging wearily</u>, the exhausted zombies couldn't have caught the humans in the sports car.
    a.  noun phrase
    b.  verb phrase
    c.  prepositional phrase
    d.  participial phrase
    e.  infinitive phrase

2.  Trudging wearily, <u>the exhausted</u> zombies couldn't have caught the humans in the sports car.
    a.  noun phrase
    b.  verb phrase
    c.  prepositional phrase
    d.  participial phrase
    e.  infinitive phrase

3.  Trudging wearily, the exhausted zombies <u>couldn't have caught the humans</u> in the sports car.
    a.  noun phrase
    b.  verb phrase
    c.  prepositional phrase
    d.  participial phrase
    e.  infinitive phrase

4.  <u>At midnight</u>, dozens of sleepy people were awakened by the
    noise and wondered what had happened.
    a.  noun phrase
    b.  verb phrase
    c.  prepositional phrase
    d.  participial phrase
    e.  infinitive phrase

5.  If you want <u>to get good grades</u>, make sure you do the readings
    and the homework.
    a.  noun phrase
    b.  verb phrase
    c.  prepositional phrase
    d.  participial phrase
    e.  infinitive phrase

**KEY FOR PRACTICE EXERCISE 5.6**

1.  d
2.  a
3.  b
4.  c
5.  e

## 5.7 Complements

A linking verb (see section 6.7) takes a subject complement instead of a
direct object. Complements can be single words, phrases, or entire clauses,
but the important thing is that they are telling you more about the subject.

*This bracket is what you need to fix the shelf.*
The verb *is* links the complement, *what you need*, with the subject, *bracket*.

*After the coach made them run wind sprints, the players were exhausted.*
The verb *were* links the complement, *exhausted*, with the subject, *players*.
Notice that the first clause, *After the coach made them run wind sprints*, has
a direct object, *wind sprints*—it's okay to have both in a complex sentence.

---

**PRACTICE EXERCISE 5.7**

## COMPLEMENTS

Underline the complement in each sentence.

1. I look incredible in my granddad's old uniform.

2. Her goulash tastes terrible because she doesn't use enough paprika.

3. She overcame an abusive childhood, got an education, and became the head surgeon.

4. When I grow old, I shall wear the bottoms of my trousers rolled.

5. Bruce Springsteen is truly the boss.

**KEY FOR PRACTICE EXERCISE 5.7**

1. incredible
2. terrible
3. the head surgeon
4. old
5. the boss

## 5.8 Misplaced Modifiers

Misplaced modifiers are phrases too far away from whatever they are supposed to modify. These can be hard to spot because you often know what people *meant*, even if that's not what they *wrote*. Regardless, it's good practice to make sure modifiers are in the right place. Be especially careful of adverbs and phrases referring to time.

> *The Senate Judiciary Committee will confront the administration over the practice of targeted killings at a hearing Tuesday.*
> This makes it sound as if the targeted killings happened at a hearing Tuesday because that phrase comes after *the targeted killings* rather than after *confront the administration. At a hearing Tuesday* could also go at the very beginning of the sentence.

> *Having finished dessert, the waitstaff cleared the plates away.*
> Did the waitstaff finish the dessert? No, the diners did, but they aren't even mentioned in the sentence. This is a specific kind of misplaced modifier called a **dangler**—it "dangles" because it can't hook on to anything in the sentence. The sentence needs to be rewritten; two possibilities are *After the diners finished dessert, the waitstaff cleared the plates away* or *Having finished dessert, the diners asked the waitstaff to clear the plates away.*

To spot and fix misplaced modifiers, carefully check lead-ins and time phrases to make sure they're next to whatever they're modifying.

## MISPLACED MODIFIERS

Underline the misplaced modifier in each sentence.

1. The senators are downplaying the assault weapons ban in the gun violence package put together after December's mass shooting by the president's handpicked task force.

2. The prosecutor announced that the suspect had been charged with murder during a news conference downtown.

3. After 95 years of working the land, it's clear that the best foods come from the best ingredients.

4. We will honor three veteran journalists for their dedication to accurate and honest reporting at the Capitol Hill Club.

5. When reorganizing your business, employees must trust that you have a clear destination in mind and that you are committed to progress.

**KEY FOR PRACTICE EXERCISE 5.8**

1. by the president's handpicked task force (This makes it sound as if the task force did the mass shooting when, in fact, they put together the gun violence package.)

2. during a news conference downtown (This makes it sound as if the murder happened at the news conference when, in fact, the announcement was made at the news conference.)

3. After 95 years of working the land (Who is working the land?)

4. at the Capitol Hill Club (We can assume that the journalists reported from more places than the club, which is where they will be honored.)

5. When reorganizing your business (This makes it sound as if the employees are reorganizing your business, when in fact, you are.)

## 5.9 Parallel Construction

With lists or with constructions such as *either . . . or*, *both . . . and*, and *not only . . . but also*, you need to make sure that the elements in each part are **parallel**, or structured the same. For example, each element should be a noun phrase, or each should be a clause. To make this easy to see, break out the elements as bullet points and make sure they've got the same structure.

*The city is dealing with locally produced ozone, pollution from the Gulf Coast, and prairie burns cause high levels of smoke.*

Make the elements into bullets:

*The city is dealing with*

- *locally produced ozone,*
- *pollution from the Gulf Coast, and*
- *prairie burns cause high levels of smoke.*

The base of the first element is the noun *ozone*, the second element is the noun *pollution*, but the third element is a clause: *burns cause*. This means that the construction is not parallel. You can fix this by making the last element into a noun modified by either a relative clause or a participial phrase:

*. . . and prairie burns <u>that</u> cause high levels of smoke.*

*. . . and prairie burns <u>causing</u> high levels of smoke.*

With correlative conjunctions (see section 14.2), make sure that whatever comes after each part is parallel. So, for instance, if you put a verb after *either*, make sure you also have one after *or*: Instead of *We will have to find the book <u>either at the library or go buy a copy</u>*, try *We will have to <u>either get the book at the library or go buy a copy</u>.*

# PARALLEL CONSTRUCTION

Identify whether each sentence is parallel or not. If not, fix the sentence so it's parallel.

1. Natural gas prices have fallen, which not only affects the price homeowners pay for gas but also the price of electricity produced by gas power plants.
   ___ Parallel
   ___ Not parallel.
   Fix: _____
   _____

2. Many victims of the bombings died, were seriously injured, or lost limbs.
   ___ Parallel
   ___ Not parallel.
   Fix: _____
   _____

3. We need to either get those books from the library or see if they're online.
   ___ Parallel
   ___ Not parallel.
   Fix: _____
   _____

4. The coach said the players needed to work on fundamentals, offense, and try to handle the ball better.
   ___ Parallel
   ___ Not parallel.
   Fix: _____
   _____

5. The professor objected to both the structure of the article and it was poorly written.

___ Parallel

___ Not parallel.

Fix: _____

_____

## KEY FOR PRACTICE EXERCISE 5.9

1. Not parallel (Fix by moving "affects" so it goes with both elements of the "not only . . . but also" phrase: Natural gas prices have fallen, which affects not only the price homeowners pay for gas but also the price of electricity produced by gas power plants.)

2. Parallel

3. Parallel

4. Not parallel (Fix by turning the last element into a noun: The coach said the players needed to work on fundamentals, offense, and ball handling.)

5. Not parallel (Fix by turning the last element into a noun: The professor objected to both the structure of the article and its poor writing. *Or* restructure so each element has a verb: The professor both objected to the structure of the article and said it was poorly written.)

## QUIZ FOR CHAPTER 5: SENTENCE STRUCTURE

For questions 1–5, refer to the following sentence and match the element with its role:

**The village was deserted, except for journalists in a dusty tent and Syrian army soldiers who were dismantling explosives.**

| | | |
|---|---|---|
| 1. | village | **direct object** |
| 2. | who were dismantling explosives | **prepositional phrase** |
| 3. | deserted | **subject** |
| 4. | in a dusty tent | **relative clause** |
| 5. | explosives | **complement** |

For questions 6–10, refer to the following sentence:

**The company's long struggle—not to mention the millions of dollars that it spent—highlight the need for drastic reforms to the system.**

6. What is the subject of the sentence?
   a. company
   b. struggle
   c. millions
   d. reforms

7. Does the subject of the sentence agree with the verb?
   a. yes
   b. no

8. What is the direct object of the sentence?
   a. company
   b. dollars
   c. need
   d. reforms

9.   Which of the following is *not* an object of a preposition?

   a.  struggle

   b.  dollars

   c.  reforms

   d.  system

10.  What is the relative clause in the sentence?

   a.  company's long struggle

   b.  millions of dollars

   c.  that it spent

   d.  reforms to the system

For questions 11–15, identify whether the clause is independent or dependent.

11.  Why do the stars shine?

   **independent    dependent**

12.  Since you moved to Detroit

   **independent    dependent**

13.  We can figure it out

   **independent    dependent**

14.  Because a bird was squawking all night

   **independent    dependent**

15.  Wild horses are facing drought and losing their habitat

   **independent    dependent**

For questions 16–20, indicate the role of the underlined phrase.

16.  <u>The tall, dark stranger</u> turned out to be the hero.
   a.  participial phrase
   b.  prepositional phrase
   c.  verb phrase
   d.  noun phrase
   e.  infinitive phrase

17.  She <u>would have offered</u> him a second chance if he'd asked.
   a.  participial phrase
   b.  prepositional phrase
   c.  verb phrase
   d.  noun phrase
   e.  infinitive phrase

18.  <u>To grasp</u> quantum mechanics takes years of study.
   a.  participial phrase
   b.  prepositional phrase
   c.  verb phrase
   d.  noun phrase
   e.  infinitive phrase

19.  <u>Angered by the rude fans</u>, the athlete walked off the field.
   a.  participial phrase
   b.  prepositional phrase
   c.  verb phrase
   d.  noun phrase
   e.  infinitive phrase

20. She had a craving <u>for a big, juicy steak</u>.
    a. participial phrase
    b. prepositional phrase
    c. verb phrase
    d. noun phrase
    e. infinitive phrase

For questions 21–25, mark whether the sentence has a misplaced modifier, nonparallel construction, or no error.

21. The nurse who was treated for Ebola spoke at a news conference as members of her nursing staff looked on after being discharged from the hospital.
    **misplaced modifier**    **nonparallel construction**    **no error**

22. The salon's services include haircuts, coloring, and it offers manicures and pedicures.
    **misplaced modifier**    **nonparallel construction**    **no error**

23. Facing a severe budget shortfall, it's easy to see how online services might fill the gap.
    **misplaced modifier**    **nonparallel construction**    **no error**

24. If the mayor supports the parking exemption, no one will be able to find a spot on the north side of campus.
    **misplaced modifier**    **nonparallel construction**    **no error**

25. We need to tidy up the backyard, the shed, and trim the front hedges.
    **misplaced modifier**    **nonparallel construction**    **no error**

---

*Answers can be found on page 197.*

# 6.0
## VERBS

WORDS

**Y**ou probably learned in school that verbs are "action words," and that's true. But verbs can also indicate conditions, connections, or other things that happen that aren't quite "actions."

This chapter will take you through all the information verbs can convey and show you how to choose the right verb form for what you want to say.

## 6.1 Conjugation

Verbs change according to a process called **conjugation**. Conjugation involves changes in the base verb as well as the addition of **auxiliary verbs**, also called "helping verbs," to convey information other than simply what's happening, such as who's doing it or to whom it's being done, when it happened, whether it's finished, whether it's possible or obligatory or hypothetical, and so on.

English verbs have three main forms, also called **principal parts**: the base or infinitive (*to ___*) form, the past tense form, and the past participle form. Verbs also have a present participle, or *-ing*, form, which shows up with some auxiliary verbs as well as in participles and gerunds.

For regular verbs, the principal parts are base/*-ed*/*-ed*, such as *talk/talked/talked*. The *-ed* and *-ing* endings join directly to the verb. When a verb ends in *e*, the final *e* usually drops out in the present participle form: *invade/invading*. If a one-syllable verb ends in a single consonant, that consonant usually doubles before the ending: *bat/batted/batting*. For multisyllable verbs ending in a single consonant, that consonant usually does *not* double in American English: *travel/traveled/traveling*.

For irregular verbs—and English has a lot of these—the principal parts depend on what language the verb came from, when it entered English, and so on, but they don't follow a pattern. So we get *ring/rang/rung* but *bring/brought/brought* and *go/went/gone* but *do/did/done*. Most dictionaries list verb forms and their preferred spellings, so if you're not sure, look it up.

Auxiliary verbs are forms of *be*, *have*, and *do* and combine with other verb forms. *Be* and *have* forms mark tense, aspect, and voice (see sections 6.4

and 6.6), whereas *do* forms indicate emphasis or questions with verbs that don't normally have an auxiliary: *Did you read the paper? Don't you know her?* Other auxiliary forms are modals (see section 6.8), which add an extra layer of meaning.

---

**PRACTICE EXERCISE 6.1**

## CONJUGATION

Fill in the missing verb forms. Use a dictionary if you need to.

| Base form | Past tense | Past participle | Present participle |
|---|---|---|---|
| 1. to teach | _____ | _____ | _____ |
| 2. _____ | liked | _____ | _____ |
| 3. _____ | _____ | sung | _____ |
| 4. _____ | _____ | _____ | going |
| 5. to cover | _____ | _____ | _____ |

**KEY FOR PRACTICE EXERCISE 6.1**

1. to teach/taught/taught/teaching
2. to like/liked/liked/liking
3. to sing/sang/sung/singing
4. to go/went/gone/going
5. to cover/covered/covered/covering

## 6.2 Person

A verb's "person" is simply the subject of the verb from the point of view of the speaker or writer.

- First person is the speaker or writer: *I* or *we*
- Second person is the listener or reader: *you*
- Third person is everyone and everything else

Most professional writing, journalism, research papers, reports, and nonfiction books are written in third person. The author doesn't use *I* and doesn't address the reader directly because the focus is on the information.

*Online news sources are trying to discourage the use of ad blockers.*

*Steven Pinker writes books on psychology and language.*

For more casual writing, such as blog or social media posts, or in instructional books such as this one, it's common to see writing from the second person perspective because the writer's intention is to engage with "you," the reader.

*You can bet the trash talk is only going to get worse.*

*If you really wanted to go, you wouldn't have waited so long to buy a ticket.*

Fiction, memoirs, and personal essays are often written in first person, using *I*, when someone wants to tell a story from a personal point of view.

*Last night I dreamt I went to Manderley again.*

*Everywhere we turn, we see people staring at their phones.*

**PRACTICE EXERCISE 6.2**

# PERSON

Identify whether the verb is first, second, or third person in each sentence.

1. If you like that shirt, then you should buy two.
   **first   second   third**

2. I wrote that paper a year ago.
   **first   second   third**

3. Jealousy, according to Shakespeare, is a "green-eyed monster."
   **first   second   third**

4. She is the youngest of seven sisters.
   **first   second   third**

5. When you think of the meaning of life, what do you think of?
   **first   second   third**

**KEY FOR PRACTICE EXERCISE 6.2**

1. second person (you like; you should)
2. first person (I wrote)
3. third person (jealousy is)
4. third person (She is)
5. second person (you think)

## 6.3 Number

A verb's "number" is how many subjects are involved.

- Singular means one person or thing is the subject of the verb.
- Plural means more than one person or thing is the subject.

Number is important because verbs can have different forms for singular and plural, and, as we mentioned in the last chapter, the verb and the subject need to match, or "agree," in number.

You find the singular/plural distinction most often in third person present tense verbs. In regular verbs, only the third person singular form adds an -s:

*I scream, you scream, we all scream for ice cream. She screams for ice cream.*

With irregular verbs, the forms may change a bit differently:

*Amanda has a nice car. Her parents have two other cars.*

*Matt does yoga with me. We do yoga three times a week.*

With *to be*, the forms change a lot differently and go beyond the third person:

*Miguel is supposed to do the dishes. I am supposed to help, and you are, too.*

**PRACTICE EXERCISE 6.3**

# NUMBER

In each sentence, identify whether the verb is singular or plural.

1. My sister wears pink on Wednesdays.
   **singular   plural**

2. On Wednesdays, we wear pink.
   **singular   plural**

3. Your friend here is only mostly dead.
   **singular   plural**

4. They were looking for two droids.
   **singular   plural**

5. I am waiting for it to stop raining.
   **singular   plural**

**KEY FOR PRACTICE EXERCISE 6.3**

1. singular (my sister wears)
2. plural (we wear)
3. singular (your friend is)
4. plural (they were looking)
5. singular (I am waiting)

## 6.4 Aspect and Tense

These two characteristics of a verb are intertwined in English, so it's best to look at them together. A verb's "aspect" indicates whether an action is finished or ongoing. A verb's "tense" shows when the action took place.

Auxiliary verbs and suffixes combine to indicate a verb's aspect and tense. With four aspects and three tenses, forms multiply pretty quickly, but they do each have a particular role and meaning: a general state, a continuing action, something that started in one time frame and is ongoing into another, or something done in one time frame that's relevant to another. Not all verbs have all tense-aspect combinations. Contractions are common with forms that include auxiliary verbs.

### 6.4.1 PRESENT TENSE: THIS IS SOMETHING HAPPENING NOW.

- *Simple present* is for a general statement, and it's just the base form of the verb, with no auxiliary:

  *I like tacos. I make them a lot. I buy them from a food truck, too.*

- *Present progressive* is for an ongoing action and is formed with the present tense of *be* plus the *-ing* form of the verb:

  *She is reading the works of Dostoevsky this summer.*

- *Present perfect* is something that was completed in the past but is relevant in the present. It's formed with the present tense of *have* plus the past participle form of the verb:

  *Now that you have finished your essay, let's go out!*

- *Present perfect progressive* is for ongoing actions that started in the past and are still going on now. It's formed with the present tense of *have* plus *been* plus the *-ing* form of the verb:

  *They have been living in Kansas for more than a decade.*

### 6.4.2. PAST TENSE: THIS IS SOMETHING THAT ALREADY HAPPENED.

- *Simple past* makes a general statement that something happened and is just the past tense form of the verb, with no auxiliaries:

  *I <u>loved</u> that book. Alyssa <u>built</u> the shelves. We <u>did</u> it!*

- *Past progressive* is for an ongoing action, usually something that was interrupted when something else happened. It's formed with the past tense of *be* plus the *-ing* form of the verb:

  *My family <u>was watching</u> a movie when the tornado sirens went off.*

- *Past perfect* (sometimes referred to as *pluperfect* if you're reading old-timey grammar books or taking Latin) is for actions that were completed in the past before something else in the past that you're talking about. It's formed with *had* plus the *-ed*/past participle form of the verb:

  *Luckily, we <u>had cleaned</u> the office before the CEO's surprise visit.*

- *Past perfect progressive* is for an action that was ongoing in the past before it stopped when something else in the past happened. This is formed with *had been* plus the *-ing* form of the verb:

  *The team <u>had been working</u> on this project for over a month when it got canceled.*

### 6.4.3 FUTURE TENSE: THIS IS SOMETHING THAT'S GOING TO HAPPEN AT A LATER TIME.

- *Simple future* makes a general statement that something will happen. It's formed one of two ways: *will* plus the base form of the verb, or the present tense of *be* plus *going to* plus the base form of the verb.

  *I <u>will be</u> back. I <u>am</u> not <u>going to give</u> up.*

Note #1: The present progressive is often used with a simple future meaning, usually when the action is happening soon or at a specified time: *We are meeting them after work. My colleagues are flying to Chicago for the conference. Carly is graduating in May.*

Note #2: The auxiliary *shall* was traditionally used instead of *will* with first person verbs, but now it's largely confined to legal/obligatory uses and formal suggestions/requests like "Shall we dance?"

- *Future progressive* is for something ongoing in the future. It's formed with *will* plus *be* plus the *-ing* form of the verb:

  *I'd love to go but I will be working all weekend.*

- *Future perfect* indicates that at a time in the future, something will be done. This is formed with *will have* plus the *-ed*/past participle form of the verb:

  *Hopefully, Jared will have finished his homework before you get here.*

- *Future perfect progressive* is for an ongoing action in the future that ties into another future action. It's formed with *will have been* plus the *-ing* form of the verb.

  *By the time they catch up, we will have been looking for several hours already.*

**PRACTICE EXERCISE 6.4**

## ASPECT AND TENSE

Put a check mark in the boxes that indicate the correct aspect and tense of the verb in each sentence.

| Verb | Aspect | | | Tense | | |
|---|---|---|---|---|---|---|
| | Simple | Perfect | Progressive | Present | Past | Future |
| 1. We're **going to rock** this party. | | | | | | |
| 2. Security cameras **are watching** everyone in the building. | | | | | | |
| 3. I**'ve** never **been** to Los Angeles, but I**'ve been** to San Francisco. | | | | | | |
| 4. I **ran** away from the scary clowns. | | | | | | |
| 5. The dog **was barking** at two men who **were walking** past the house. | | | | | | |

KEY FOR PRACTICE EXERCISE 6.4

1.   ✓ simple      ✓ future
2.   ✓ present     ✓ progressive
3.   ✓ present     ✓ perfect
4.   ✓ simple      ✓ past
5.   ✓ past        ✓ progressive

## 6.5 Mood

A verb's "mood" reflects the speaker's perspective on the contents of the sentence. There are three moods: indicative, subjunctive, and imperative.

**Indicative mood** is the most common. It states a fact, asks a question, or expresses an opinion: *You bought the blue dress. What made you choose the blue one? I think you look great!*

**Subjunctive mood** is used for hypothetical and contrary-to-fact situations, as well as for wishes and requests.

*If it hadn't rained (but it did), we would have gone to the park (but we didn't).*

*I wish I knew how to speak Japanese (but I don't).*

The somewhat complicated rules for verb tense with subjunctives have been undergoing a simplification as the language changes. The best advice for now is to trust your ear and don't overthink it. Remember that verbs are usually in the past tense (but not with *let* subjunctives), and *could*, *would*, and *should* show up a lot. Think of *If I were you* and let that be your model.

Also, be careful to distinguish a subjunctive from a conditional, which is indicative: A conditional *could* happen; a subjunctive *didn't* or *won't*.

*If you build it, they will come.*

**Imperative mood** expresses a command: *Get out of this house! Entertain us. Stop at red lights. Don't talk to strangers.* The subject (you) is understood but usually omitted.

---

**PRACTICE EXERCISE 6.5**

## MOOD

Identify the mood of the verb in each sentence.

1.  If I were an editor, I wouldn't need this book.
    **indicative   subjunctive   imperative**

2.  Call me when you want to talk.
    **indicative   subjunctive   imperative**

3.  When I get to the end of a book, I start another one.
    **indicative   subjunctive   imperative**

4.  I don't care if it rains tonight.
    **indicative   subjunctive   imperative**

5.  She wished she knew how to play a musical instrument.
    **indicative   subjunctive   imperative**

**KEY FOR PRACTICE EXERCISE 6.5**

1.  subjunctive (hypothetical *if*)
2.  imperative
3.  indicative
4.  indicative (conditional *if*—it could happen)
5.  subjunctive

## 6.6 Voice

A verb's "voice" indicates the focus of the action: who's doing it or who is having it done to them. The two voices are **active** and **passive**.

Active voice is simple subject-verb or subject-verb-object structure (see section 5.3), where the subject is doing the verb:

*We're <u>studying</u> for the exam.*

*We <u>study</u> engineering.*

*We <u>ordered</u> pizza.*

*We'll <u>eat</u> in a half hour.*

Passive voice takes the direct object and makes it the subject, with the verb being done to the subject. The original subject is sometimes put into a *by* phrase:

Active: *The cat ate the tuna.* Passive: *The tuna <u>was eaten</u> by the cat.*

Active: *Her bridesmaids wore green dresses.* Passive: *Green dresses <u>were worn</u> by her bridesmaids.*

Passives can sometimes be wordy or too indirect for what you want to say. They can also be deliberately vague when no *by* phrase is included:

*Mistakes <u>were made</u>.* (No one gets the blame with this sentence.)

But passive voice is perfectly grammatical and is sometimes the right choice, especially when who does the action isn't as important or is unknown:

*The First National Bank <u>was robbed</u> yesterday.* (We don't know yet who did it, and the important thing is that the bank was robbed.)

*A suspect in the robbery <u>was arrested</u> this morning.* (Obviously, police arrest people. But the important thing here is that a suspect is in custody.)

One piece of writing advice you may have heard is "Avoid the passive voice." That's not bad advice, but as the examples above show, sometime passive is the best choice. Also, make sure you've correctly identified a passive voice verb. Passive voice is not the same as a linking verb (see next section) or a verb phrase that includes auxiliary verbs. Passives occur only with verbs that can take a direct object, called transitive verbs (see next section).

---

**PRACTICE EXERCISE 6.6**

## VOICE

In each sentence, identify whether the verb is active or passive.

1. The weather seems unstable today.
   **active   passive**

2. Hail is falling from the sky.
   **active   passive**

3. The dogs are frightened by thunder.
   **active   passive**

4. We'll have to clean up the yard.
   **active   passive**

5. A bunch of tree limbs were knocked down in the storm.
   **active   passive**

**KEY FOR PRACTICE EXERCISE 6.6**

1. active
2. active
3. passive
4. active
5. passive

## 6.7 Action Verbs and Linking Verbs

Verbs can be either **action verbs** or **linking verbs**. Action verbs are "doing" verbs; linking verbs are "being" verbs. The difference is in the predicate (see section 5.1): Linking verbs connect the subject to the predicate. Action verbs can stand alone or have something else in the predicate, such as a direct object or prepositional phrase.

Action verbs can be **transitive** or **intransitive**. All these two fancy terms do is distinguish verbs that take a direct object (see section 5.3) from verbs that don't. Transitive verbs have a direct object: something in the sentence that the action is done to. Here, it's *cake*:

*Cade likes cake. He eats cake every chance he gets. He bakes cakes, too.*

Action verbs can also be intransitive—they don't have a direct object but are still talking about an action.

*Molly runs every morning. She has been running since grade school.*

Many action verbs can be either transitive or intransitive, depending on the sentence:

*Olga just read* War and Peace. (Transitive: direct object is *War and Peace.*)
*She reads daily.* (Intransitive: predicate is just verb + adverb.)

Linking verbs, on the other hand, are always intransitive. They have subject complements (see section 5.7) instead of direct objects.

*Cade will be a master chef someday. Molly looks very fit. Olga seems intelligent.*

### PRACTICE EXERCISE 6.7

## ACTION VERBS AND LINKING VERBS

In each sentence, identify whether the verb is an action verb or a linking verb.

1. She seems really happy right now.

   **action   linking**

2. The club bicycled to the next town and back.

   **action   linking**

3. The dog ate an entire pizza.

   **action   linking**

4. My aunt became a biochemical researcher.

   **action   linking**

5. We want progress and we want it now!

   **action   linking**

### KEY FOR PRACTICE EXERCISE 6.7

1. linking
2. action
3. action
4. linking
5. action

## 6.8 Modal Verbs

Modals are a group of auxiliary verbs that let you know something is possible, allowed, suggested, or necessary. These are "coulda, woulda, shoulda" verbs. They include the following:

**Ability/possibility/permission:** *can, could, may, might*
**Obligation/suggestion:** *should, shall, ought to, would, will*
**Necessity:** *must, need to, have to*

With a modal, verb forms that normally change to indicate person (see section 6.2) don't change:

*He <u>could go</u> with us to the movie.*

*We <u>should ask</u> him.*

*Whatever we decide, we <u>need to leave</u> by 6:30 p.m.*

For past tense modals, use the past participle form of the main verb:

*He <u>might have wanted</u> to come with us.*

*We <u>should have asked</u> him sooner.*

*We <u>must have done</u> something to upset him!*

Some dialects double up modals, as in "We *might could* go get a burger" or "She *shouldn't ought to* say things like that." Although these are fine in conversation, it's best not to use them in academic or professional writing.

## PRACTICE EXERCISE 6.8

### MODAL VERBS

In each sentence, fill in the correct form of the main verb given in parentheses.

1.  I don't know where Helen is, but I think she might have _____ on vacation. (go)

2.  Everyone said they should have _____ a cleaner campaign. (run)

3.  Could you _____ whether the scouts need any help? (see)

4.  We need to have _____ all the chairs over before the party. (bring)

5.  Be careful—burnt popcorn can _____ up the whole office! (stink)

### KEY FOR PRACTICE EXERCISE 6.8

1.  gone
2.  run
3.  see
4.  brought
5.  stink

## 6.9 Consistent Tense and Sequence of Tenses

One of the pitfalls in writing, especially for beginners and in creative writing, is not keeping the verb tense consistent. All this means is that if you start writing with present tense, keep it in present, and if you start in past tense, keep it in past. It's distracting to readers if you jump back and forth between present and past, or present and future.

One instance where the tense can change is in reported speech. This is called **sequence of tenses** and comes into play when you're not directly quoting someone but instead relaying to someone else what they told you. Something said in the past about the present is reported in the past tense, something said in the past about the past is reported in the past perfect, and something said in the past about the future is reported with a modal. Here are some examples:

*"I see a hundred birds in the yard," John said.*
*John <u>said he saw</u> a hundred birds in the yard.*

*"I saw them yesterday, too," John said.*
*John <u>said he had seen</u> them yesterday, too.*

*"I will come tonight to see the birds," Mary Kay said.*
*Mary Kay <u>said she would</u> come tonight to see the birds.*

So-called universal truths are an exception to this—these are things that don't change, that are ongoing, that are intrinsic to a person or place, and so on. Compare these sentences:

*Frank said his father was an electrical engineer.*
*Frank said his father was a kind, funny man.*

With the first sentence, readers will assume the father is simply retired. With the second, because it's in the past and dealing with something essential to a person, readers will assume the father is deceased.

Also, if there is a contrast between past and present, leave the present in the present tense:

*Jeff <u>said he loved</u> mushroom pizza in college but <u>hates</u> mushrooms now.*

Don't overthink sequence of tenses: Trust your ear; it'll be right most of the time.

**PRACTICE EXERCISE 6.9**

## CONSISTENT TENSE

In each sentence, fill in the correct form of the verb in parentheses.

1.  He said he _____ (think) what he did _____ (is) the right thing to do.

2.  The teacher said a circle _____ (have) 360 degrees.

3.  Mom promised she _____ (go) to the store after work tomorrow.

4.  The Jeffersons said they _____ (enjoy) their trip to Australia last year.

5.  She said *The Catcher in the Rye* _____ (is) her favorite book.

**KEY FOR PRACTICE EXERCISE 6.9**

1.  thought; was
2.  has
3.  would go
4.  enjoyed
5.  is

## 6.10 Phrasal Verbs

English loves adding prepositions to verbs to change the meaning. When that happens, they're called **phrasal verbs** because the verb itself is a phrase. The prepositions that stick to the verbs function more like adverbs, meaning that they don't necessarily have to have an object.

*I don't know how to <u>set up</u> my new <u>Wi-Fi</u> router.*

*My old <u>Wi-Fi</u> router <u>broke down</u>.*

Phrasal verbs can also be split—that is, other words can come between the verb and the preposition:

*I just can't <u>figure</u> her <u>out</u>.*

*Please <u>throw</u> your trash <u>away</u> before leaving the picnic area.*

---

**PRACTICE EXERCISE 6.10**

# PHRASAL VERBS

Match the phrasal verb with the sentence in which it fits best.

1. The kids need to _____ all their toys before bed.                   *put back*

2. Did you _____ the cat this morning?            *put up with*

3. Annie, _____ that candy! We're not buying treats today!              *put away*

4. She asked the shop to _____ some flounder for her.              *put out*

5. How do you _____ all that noise?               *put aside*

*(continued)*

*(continued)*

**KEY FOR PRACTICE EXERCISE 6.10**

1. put away
2. put out
3. put back
4. put aside
5. put up with

## 6.11 Verbals

Verbs have some forms that act like other parts of speech. These are called **verbals** and include participles, gerunds, and infinitives.

**Participles** are verbs that act like adjectives. A lot of participles are so common as adjectives that we don't even think of them as verbs: *the chosen one, an interesting book, a compelling story, an undiscovered manuscript.* English has active participles and passive participles. Active participles are the *-ing* form of the verb; passive participles are the third principle part (see section 6.1), ending in *-ed* or an irregular form.

**Gerunds** are verbs that act like nouns. They can be subjects, direct objects, or objects of prepositions. They are always the *-ing* form of the verb: *Michael Phelps is really good at swimming. The park offers hiking and biking. Cooking is their hobby.*

**Infinitives** are the *to* form of the verb. They also function as nouns and often head up a whole phrase: *To write like a professional, learn the rules.* Perfect infinitives are formed with *to have* plus the past participle form and indicate action prior to the rest of the sentence: *To have lived in Beirut then, must have been harrowing.* Passive infinitives are the passive forms of transitive verbs, formed with *to be* (present) or *to have been* (past) plus the past participle form: *To have been taken from her family at such a young age must have been traumatic for Lucy.*

**PRACTICE EXERCISE 6.11**

## VERBALS

In each sentence, indicate whether the underlined verbal is a gerund, participle, or infinitive.

1. To be or not to be, that is the question.
   **gerund   participle   infinitive**

2. Spurs jangling, the cowboy walked up to the bar.
   **gerund   participle   infinitive**

3. Horseback riding is her one passion.
   **gerund   participle   infinitive**

4. The group's main goal is hacking into the CIA's computers.
   **gerund   participle   infinitive**

5. The bound volumes of newspapers are in the basement.
   **gerund   participle   infinitive**

**KEY FOR PRACTICE EXERCISE 6.11**

1. infinitive
2. participle
3. gerund
4. gerund
5. participle

## QUIZ FOR CHAPTER 6: VERBS

For questions 1–20, choose the description that identifies the underlined verb.

1. I'll tell you what <u>I want</u>: a new car.
   a. first person
   b. second person
   c. third person

2. <u>You don't know</u> my cousin, but she's great.
   a. first person
   b. second person
   c. third person

3. The sun <u>is</u> in my eyes.
   a. singular
   b. plural

4. Where <u>were</u> my friends when I needed them?
   a. singular
   b. plural

5. Who'<u>ll be able to lead this group</u>?
   a. simple present
   b. present progressive
   c. simple future
   d. future perfect

6. The Allies <u>had</u> just <u>won</u> the war.
   a. simple past
   b. past perfect
   c. past progressive
   d. past perfect progressive

7.   I've been walking to work instead of driving.

   a.  simple present

   b.  present perfect

   c.  present progressive

   d.  present perfect progressive

8.   I wish you were here to see this!

   a.  indicative

   b.  subjunctive

   c.  imperative

9.   I've got some money.

   a.  indicative

   b.  subjunctive

   c.  imperative

10.  Go on, take another piece.

   a.  indicative

   b.  subjunctive

   c.  imperative

11.  He wrote a poem, and it is called "Yellow Sunrise."

   a.  active

   b.  passive

12.  He wrote a poem, and it is called "Yellow Sunrise."

   a.  active

   b.  passive

13.  Her joy in life seems faded.

   a.  action verb

   b.  linking verb

14.  I ate dinner in a fancy restaurant.

   a.  action verb

   b.  linking verb

15. You <u>can</u> check out up to 12 books at a time, but you <u>can</u> have them for only two weeks.
    a. modal
    b. subjunctive
    c. gerund
    d. participle

16. If they say we can't meet there, then where <u>will we go</u>?
    a. indicative
    b. modal
    c. gerund
    d. participle

17. <u>Choose</u> a kitten that likes to purr.
    a. participle
    b. modal
    c. subjunctive
    d. imperative

18. <u>Sailing</u> is a sport that requires a lot of money.
    a. participle
    b. modal
    c. gerund
    d. imperative

19. After the burglary, <u>shattered</u> glass was strewn all over the kitchen floor.
    a. modal
    b. participle
    c. gerund
    d. infinitive

20. If you can't write well, it will be hard <u>to find</u> a job.
    a. modal
    b. participle
    c. gerund
    d. infinitive

For questions 21–25, fill in the correct form of the verb in parentheses. You may need to add an auxiliary verb.

21. "I _____ that's a good idea," she said. (think)

22. Yesterday she said she _____ it was a good idea. (think)

23. When we rang the doorbell, they _____ just _____ the dishes. (finish)

24. If I _____ rich, I'd travel the world. (is)

25. While the plane was sitting on the tarmac with the gate in sight, the passengers _____ increasingly annoyed. (grow)

_____

*Answers can be found on page 198.*

# 7.0

## DETERMINERS

WORDS

Determiners are a special kind of modifier. They come at the front of a noun phrase and tell us what the noun is referring to or in relation to, and whether it's specific or general. Determiners fall into several categories: articles, demonstratives, possessives, quantifiers, and interrogatives.

The only **articles** are *the* and *a/an*. *The* is the **definite article**, which means that you are talking about a noun that has already been mentioned or is known: *Did you bring the camera?* *A/an* is the **indefinite article**, which means that the noun is generic, unknown, or unspecified: *Do you have a camera?* Nouns don't have to have an article; more plurals than singulars (see section 8.6) will appear without one because the indefinite article can appear only with a singular noun: *They sell cameras and tripods.* Some languages—Mandarin and Russian, to name two—don't have articles, which is why many nonnative speakers of English have particular trouble deciding which articles to use in English, or whether to use one at all.

The **demonstratives**—*this, these, that, those*—point out something specific about the noun, and can contrast it with another noun, often something closer (*this*) or farther away (*that*). The distance can be figurative distance as well as physical: *Do you like this dress? I like that one better.*

**Possessives** mark who or what something belongs to or is associated with. *The company's headquarters. Her new job. Our mutual friend. The neighborhood's summer cookout.*

**Quantifiers** tell us "how much" or "how many." It might be a specific number or an amount, such as *all, most, some, few, none: There were no peaches left, but I ate two plums and some grapes.* A quantifier can also specify a segment of a group—such as *each, every, both, neither* (see section 8.4 for count versus noncount nouns).

The **interrogatives**—*what, which, whose*—ask for a specific detail: *Which car did you decide to get? What species of bird is that? Whose phone is on the table?*

Determiners can occur with regular adjectives and also with other determiners, though a noun can't have both an article and a demonstrative: *Their dog's six puppies are here (possessive + possessive + quantifier). All of the six puppies are female (quantifier + article + quantifier).*

## QUIZ FOR CHAPTER 7: DETERMINERS

Identify the type of determiner in each sentence.

1. Some people just don't "get" musical theater.

   **article demonstrative possessive quantifier interrogative**

2. The porch needs sweeping.

   **article demonstrative possessive quantifier interrogative**

3. That boy is trouble on wheels.

   **article demonstrative possessive quantifier interrogative**

4. Which sandwich do you want: egg salad or ham and cheese?

   **article demonstrative possessive quantifier interrogative**

5. Her policy is not to "friend" students until after graduation.

   **article demonstrative possessive quantifier interrogative**

*Answers can be found on page 198.*

# 8.0
## NOUNS

WORDS

As mentioned briefly in chapter 3, nouns are people, places, things, ideas, or concepts. There's a bit more to it than that (although not as much as with verbs), so this chapter will discuss the characteristics that nouns have, how to make them possessive or plural, and even how to turn them into verbs.

We've already seen how nouns can get another layer of meaning with determiners (see chapter 7), but determiners aren't the only words that can modify nouns. Adjectives traditionally modify nouns—*big dog*, *blue* house— and nouns themselves can work like adjectives, stacking up before a noun to add on another dimension of meaning: *bank* teller, *park* bench, *school* supplies.

## 8.1 Compound Nouns

When a noun phrase—that is, a noun with another noun, an adjective, perhaps an adverb, or a prepositional phrase—becomes so ingrained as a unit that we treat it as a single noun, we call it a **compound noun**. These occur in three ways:

- **Closed compounds:** These have fused into a single word, such as *basketball, cheeseburger,* and *website*.
- **Open compounds:** These are still individual words, although they are treated as a unit, such as *garage sale, first baseman,* and *parking lot*.
- **Hyphenated compounds:** These compounds are "stuck together" with hyphens, which show that the words function as a single unit, such *self-esteem, bird-watcher,* and *bride-to-be*.

How can we tell which compounds close, which stay open, and which get hyphenated? There's no hard-and-fast rule for this, and there's a lot of variation among style guides and dictionaries, but there are some trends. US English in particular trends toward closed compounds but not in all instances.

Compounds made up of two nouns, such as *healthcare* and *childcare,* are most likely to be closed.

Compounds made up of noun + adjective and especially noun + participle or gerund (see section 6.11), such as *upper crust* and *training exercise*, are more likely to be open.

Compounds made up of noun + "doer" noun and noun + another phrase, such as *mouth-breather* and *jack-in-the-box*, are more likely to be hyphenated.

---

**PRACTICE EXERCISE 8.1**

## COMPOUND NOUNS

Go to your usual dictionary, and after the entry for *middle*, see how it renders *middle* + the following words (look at the nouns, not adjectives):

1. age

2. school

3. ground

4. man

5. weight

**KEY FOR PRACTICE EXERCISE 8.1**

These may vary by dictionary, but probably you'll see *middle age, middle school* and *middle ground* as open compound nouns, and *middleman,* and *middleweight* as closed.

## 8.2 Possessives

When we want to indicate that someone or something belongs to or is associated with someone or something else, we use a **possessive** form.

Making nouns possessive is pretty straightforward: add apostrophe-s. For singular nouns, this is all you need to do: *Miranda's award, my brother's bike, the restaurant's specials, the class's assignment*. If the noun is plural and already ends in -s, just add an apostrophe: *the businesses' lobbyist, the candidates' debate*. If the noun is plural and doesn't already end in -s, add apostrophe-s: *children's books, people's interests*.

Only the last word of a noun phrase gets made possessive: *Peggy and Mike's boat, the University of Illinois and Northwestern's joint program*.

Sometimes possession is indicated by an *of* phrase, and generally this is used for emphasis or when it makes a string of possessives clearer, like *my best friend's sister's boyfriend's brother's girlfriend* becomes *the girlfriend of the brother of my best friend's sister's boyfriend*.

*Please* do not use apostrophe-*s* to make a noun plural. *Never.* I will remind you about this again in section 8.6 because it's that important.

---

**PRACTICE EXERCISE 8.2**

## POSSESSIVES

Make each of the following nouns possessive.

1.  author _____

2.  Missy _____

3.  The Liebermans _____

4.  Chris and Pat _____

5.  the sister of the friend of my co-worker _____

## 8.3 Collective Nouns

When a singular noun is used to indicate a group or quantity of something, it's called a **collective noun**. These are words such as *association, band, class, company, family, group, organization, staff, team*, and so on. What you need to remember is that in US English, grammar trumps meaning, and these nouns are considered singular, so use a singular verb (see section 5.2) and a singular pronoun (see section 10.4): *The team is ready for its midseason tournament.*

However, British English treats these as plural, so don't be thrown off if you see or hear something such as *Manchester have won four of their last five matches.*

If you need to emphasize the actions of individuals rather than the group, it's clearer and smoother to drop in a word such as *members*: *The agency members are preparing sections of the report. The faculty members are going to vote on the measure.* Then it's all plural and you won't run into any agreement problems.

**PRACTICE EXERCISE 8.3**

## COLLECTIVE NOUNS

In each sentence, circle the correct verbs and pronouns.

1. The corporation **is / are** expanding **its / their** product line to include mobile devices.

2. All my far-flung family members **is / are** planning to come to the reunion.

3. The navy **is / are** ready for new protocols.

4. The army installed new communications at most of **its / their** domestic bases.

5. Tell all the team members to get **its / their** stuff to the bus no later than 7 a.m.

**KEY FOR PRACTICE EXERCISE 8.3**

1. is; its
2. are
3. is
4. its
5. their

## 8.4 Count Nouns and Noncount Nouns

Nouns are also classified as **count nouns** or **noncount nouns**. As the names imply, this means that you can count count nouns, and you can't count noncount nouns. Count nouns are words such as *cars, gears, wheels, windows,* and *license plates.* You can say *many cars, six gears, four wheels, each window, few license plates.* Noncount nouns are words such as *gas, air, paint,* and *grime.* You can't say *many gas* or *five air;* you have to say *much gas* or *less air,* or add a phrase such as *a lot of: a lot of grime.*

# COUNT NOUNS AND NONCOUNT NOUNS

Identify whether each noun is a count noun or a noncount noun.

1. ocean

   **count   noncount**

2. water

   **count   noncount**

3. fish

   **count   noncount**

4. oxygen

   **count   noncount**

5. pollution

   **count   noncount**

### KEY FOR PRACTICE EXERCISE 8.4

1. count
2. noncount
3. count
4. noncount
5. noncount

## 8.5 Definite and Indefinite Articles with Nouns

Articles, as we mentioned in chapter 7, are a kind of determiner, and they fall into two categories: definite and indefinite.

The **definite article**, *the*, refers to a noun that has been specified or already mentioned or is known or important: *the president, the mayor, the books I told you about*. Definite articles can be used with singular or plural nouns.

The **indefinite article**, *a/an*, is used only in the singular and is for something unknown or unspecified: *a person came by, I see you're reading a book*. Whether you use *a* or *an* depends on the sound—not the letter—immediately following the article. If there's a consonant sound, use *a*: *a cat, a cow, a yellow flower*. If there's a vowel sound, use *an*: *an ostrich, an elephant, an MRI*. This is not complicated, but people tend to overthink words beginning in *h*. For these words, use *an* only when you do not pronounce the *h*: *a hotel, an herb sauce, a historical landmark, a hospital, a humanities class, an honorable mention*. This means that if you pronounce the *h* in *historic* and *historical*—which most of us do—it is correct to use *a*, not *an*.

Sometimes, you don't need an article at all. Noncount nouns (see the previous section) often don't take an article: *Revenge is a dish best served cold*. Nonspecific count nouns reflecting a general idea also can go article-less: *Language is complicated and often illogical*. English has a multitude of picky distinctions about articles and when to use them, which is why article use is so intuitive for native speakers but so tough for English learners.

**PRACTICE EXERCISE 8.5**

## DEFINITE AND INDEFINITE ARTICLES WITH NOUNS

In each sentence, write the appropriate article (if there should be one) in the blank.

1. These students are learning how to play _____ violin.

2. I picked up _____ ready-to-bake pizza on the way home.

3. Does your cabin have _____ electricity?

4. Would you like _____ glass of lemonade?

5. Are those _____ shoes that Kim Kardashian wore on her show?

**KEY FOR PRACTICE EXERCISE 8.5**

1. the
2. a
3. (none needed)
4. a
5. the

## 8.6 Plurals

Most nouns go from singular to plural with the addition of -*s* or -*es* on the end: *cats and dogs, places and faces, Martians and Russians.* No apostrophe, just extra letters. Add -*es* when the word ends in -*s*, -*sh*, -*ch*, -*z*, -*x*, and sometimes -*o*: *dresses, ashes, searches, buzzes, foxes, tornadoes* (but *burritos*). For nouns ending in -*y*, usually change the -*y* to -*i* and then add -*es*: *candies, pennies* (but *monkeys*).

That's easy enough, but there's a whole bushel of words in English that have irregular plural forms that don't seem to follow any rules: *mouse → mice* but *house → houses, man → men* but *can → cans, goose → geese* but *moose → moose* (more on that one in a moment), *foot → feet* but *boot → boots.* Many words ending in -*f* change the -*f* to a -*v* and then add -*es*, but not always: *thief → thieves* but *chief → chiefs, hoof → hooves* but *roof → roofs.* When in doubt, look it up: Any good dictionary lists plural forms with nouns.

There are also many, many nouns that we borrowed from Latin and Greek that have their own set of plurals, such as *vertebra → vertebrae, crisis → crises, phenomenon → phenomena, vortex → vortices,* and *candelabrum → candelabra.* Some of these we've anglicized enough that we just add -*s*, like *stadium → stadiums* (don't use *stadia* unless you want to be thought of as insufferably stuffy). Others—especially scientific or academic terms—have retained their ancient plural forms. Again, when in doubt, look it up.

Some words have the same form for both singular and plural. It may be a singular form, such as *deer* or *fish* or the above mentioned *moose,* or a plural form, such as *pants* or *glasses* (as in spectacles).

*Data* and *media* are two words that began as Latin plurals but are used in the singular with increasing frequency: *The data shows, the news media is.* In formal or academic contexts, stick to using these as plurals, but in speech and in more conversational writing, it's fine to use these words as singulars.

## PLURALS

Write the plural of each noun. Look up the word in the dictionary if you need to, but use the first plural given if you do.

1. rhinoceros

2. asteroid

3. first baseman

4. series

5. criterion

**KEY FOR PRACTICE EXERCISE 8.6**

1. rhinoceroses
2. asteroids
3. first basemen
4. series
5. criteria

# 8.7 Proper Nouns

For names of specific people, locations, entities, and products, we use **proper nouns**. These are always capitalized. Proper nouns are also used for holidays, events, and titles of creative works (books, movies, TV shows, paintings, etc.).

Proper nouns form possessives and plurals just like common (non-proper) nouns do: *Peyton Manning won two Super Bowls*. The one you probably need to watch most carefully is last names. If something belongs to one member of the family, use a singular possessive: *LeBron James's contract*. If you are talking about the whole family, make it plural, with no apostrophe:

*The James__es__ are all so proud of LeBron.* If you are talking about something that belongs to the whole family, use a plural possessive: *The Jameses' championship party was amazing*.

Make sure you don't over-capitalize. Lots of people, especially in advertising and marketing, like to Make Everything Capitalized to show you How Important it is. Unless you're writing ad copy, don't capitalize common nouns. Here's a tip that should be familiar by now: When in doubt, look it up.

---

**PRACTICE EXERCISE 8.7**

## PROPER NOUNS

Capitalize all the proper nouns in each sentence.

1. Where do you think you're going, timbuktu?

2. Two professors from the university of montana take students on an archaeological dig every summer.

3. The golden state warriors fell short in their quest for a title in 2016.

4. We won tickets to *hamilton* in a contest sponsored by the *new york times*.

5. For her summer abroad, she's going to hungary and romania to study alternative energy.

**KEY FOR PRACTICE EXERCISE 8.7**

1. Timbuktu
2. University of Montana
3. Golden State Warriors
4. *Hamilton*; *New York Times*
5. Hungary; Romania

## 8.8 "Verbing" Nouns

Nouns have a long history of being turned into verbs (and vice versa). But usually in the past, they got a verb-making suffix added, such as *energy →  energize* and *stigma → stigmatize*. But we don't have to do that—we can instead shift a noun into a verb role just as we shift it into an adjective role (see section 8.1), as with *friend, message,* and *microwave.*

Not everyone is a fan of this: Words such as *contact* and *host* started as nouns. When they shifted into verbs, they were frowned upon in many usage guides for decades before becoming accepted as mainstream. Some people still don't like *impact* as a verb meaning *affect* (*impacted* teeth are apparently fine).

The point is, "verbed" nouns often sound like jargon or buzzwords and may put people off, so be aware of your audience when deciding whether to use them.

## QUIZ FOR CHAPTER 8: NOUNS

For each noun, fill in the plural, the possessive, and the possessive plural (not all words will have all three), and indicate whether it's common or proper, and count or noncount. Feel free to use your dictionary.

| Noun | Plural | Possessive | Possessive plural | Common or proper? | Count or noncount? |
|---|---|---|---|---|---|
| 1. star | | | | | |
| 2. McLain | | | | | |
| 3. audience | | | | | |
| 4. pity | ██ | | ██ | | |
| 5. octopus | | | | | |
| 6. runner | | | | | |
| 7. Super Bowl | | | | | |
| 8. Joanna | | | | | |
| 9. hot dog | | | | | |
| 10. obesity | ██ | | ██ | | |

*Answers can be found on page 199.*

# 9.0
## ABBREVIATIONS

WORDS

bbreviations are shorter—abbreviated—forms of words and phrases. We use a lot of abbreviations every day to make our language more streamlined and to avoid having to repeat a long or cumbersome string of words. Sometimes we even borrow them from other languages: Many abbreviations, from times and dates to research citations, come from Latin. We also borrow from other languages to get abbreviations such as KGB and FIFA.

Experts in many fields have their own shorthand—abbreviations they all understand and don't need to spell out. But be aware when you are communicating, especially if you're conveying specialized information to a nonspecialist audience, that not everyone will understand certain abbreviations or interpret them in the same way, so sometimes you'll need to spell out an abbreviation at its first mention and note how you're shortening it.

## 9.1 Initialisms

Initialisms are abbreviations that use the first letter of each word in the phrase, with each letter pronounced individually, such as *FBI* or *USA*. Articles (see chapter 7: Determiners), prepositions, and conjunctions usually aren't included in the initialism. Initialisms can be in all capital letters, such as *NFL* and *MRI*, or lowercase, like *e.g.* Sometimes they include periods and sometimes they don't. And sometimes they can be rendered several ways, such as *8 AM, 8 A.M., 8 a.m.,* and *8 am.* Check your designated style guide for whether you should use periods.

Initialisms are sometimes called acronyms (see next section), but technically they're not because acronyms are pronounced as a word rather than as individual letters.

## INITIALISMS

Match each initialism with the full word or phrase.

1. talk to you later                        MLB

2. Major League Baseball           ROI

3. *id est* (that is)                        ttyl

4. mixed martial arts                    i.e.

5. return on investment              MMA

**KEY FOR PRACTICE EXERCISE 9.1**
1. ttyl
2. MLB
3. i.e.
4. MMA
5. ROI

## 9.2 Acronyms

Acronyms, like initialisms, are abbreviations that use the first letter of each word in the phrase. Unlike initialisms, they're pronounced as a word rather than a series of letters, such as *CAT scan*. Acronyms are usually written in all capital letters, such as *UNICEF* and *NASCAR*, but sometimes, when they become a part of the mainstream language, they turn lowercase, like *radar* and *snafu* (look it up). Also, some style guides require that longer acronyms have only the first letter capitalized, such as *Unicef* and *Nascar*.

**PRACTICE EXERCISE 9.2**

## ACRONYMS

Give the acronym for each full word or phrase.

1. President of the United States

2. Museum of Modern Art

3. Supplemental Nutrition Assistance Program

4. science, technology, engineering, and math

5. sound navigation and ranging

**KEY FOR PRACTICE EXERCISE 9.2**

1. POTUS
2. MOMA
3. SNAP
4. STEM
5. sonar

# 9.3 Shortened and Clipped Forms

Sometimes a word is so long that we need to shorten it. Or sometimes it's not that long at all but we shorten it anyway, so it will take only a *sec*. Isn't that *fab*? Maybe I'll write about that on my *blog*. I'll need a *pic* to go with it.

Shortened or clipped forms aren't always ultra-casual, though—some short forms are so common that we don't always realize they're short for something, like *memo* for *memorandum* or *flu* for *influenza*. But sometimes multiple words shorten the same way, so when you're writing, make sure it's clear from context what you're talking about.

PRACTICE EXERCISE 9.3

## SHORTENED AND CLIPPED FORMS

Match the clipped form with the full word or phrase.

1. quadriceps                          veggie

2. vegetable                           quads

3. veteran                             vet

4. quadruplets

5. veterinarian

6. vegetarian

**KEY FOR PRACTICE EXERCISE 9.3**

1. quads
2. veggie
3. vet
4. quads
5. vet
6. veggie

# 9.4 Portmanteaus

Portmanteaus are mash-up words, formed by combining two words into one. Sometimes they're funny and slangy, such as *adorkable* (*dorky* + *adorable*) and *bootylicious* (*booty* + *delicious*), and sometimes they go mainstream, such as *motel* (*motor* + *hotel*) and *webinar* (*web* + *seminar*). Many are tech-based, such as *malware* (*malicious* + *software*) and *modem* (*modulator* + *demodulator*).

Fun fact: A portmanteau is also a big suitcase, and we can credit author Lewis Carroll with the meaning expansion. One of his characters describes nonsense words as "like a portmanteau—there are two meanings packed up into one word."

---

**PRACTICE EXERCISE 9.4**

## PORTMANTEAUS

Combine the two words into a familiar portmanteau.

1. shopping + alcoholic = _____

2. math + athlete = _____

3. mock + documentary = _____

4. Labrador retriever + poodle = _____

5. spoon + fork = _____

**KEY FOR PRACTICE EXERCISE 9.4**

1. shopaholic
2. mathlete
3. mockumentary
4. labradoodle
5. spork

## 9.5 Pluralizing Abbreviations

As with pluralizing nouns (see section 8.6), add *-s* to make an abbreviation plural: *That store sells used video games, CDs, and DVDs.* Some style guides still say to add apostrophe-*s* to make a plural, but most mass communication style guides and some academic ones don't. Check to make sure.

Even if the final letter in the abbreviation is not for the word that would be made plural, add the *-s* to the end anyway: *The state AGs* (attorneys general) *are meeting in Nashville. Cabrera already has 50 RBIs* (runs batted in) *this season.*

---

**PRACTICE EXERCISE 9.5**

### PLURALIZING ABBREVIATIONS

Make each abbreviation plural.

1. RFP

2. doc

3. PB&J

4. cockapoo

5. MVP

**KEY FOR PRACTICE EXERCISE 9.5**

1. RFPs
2. docs
3. PB&Js
4. cockapoos
5. MVPs

## QUIZ FOR CHAPTER 9: ABBREVIATIONS

Identify the type of abbreviation in each sentence.

1.  Three NGO workers were killed in the bombing.
    **initialism   acronym   clipped form   portmanteau**

2.  We went scuba diving on our trip to the Bahamas.
    **initialism   acronym   clipped form   portmanteau**

3.  The company had its first female CEO two decades before anyone else in the industry.
    **initialism   acronym   clipped form   portmanteau**

4.  We're all meeting for brunch at 10 a.m. Sunday.
    **initialism   acronym   clipped form   portmanteau**

5.  The menu has lots of pasta dishes: spaghetti, penne, lasagna, etc.
    **initialism   acronym   clipped form   portmanteau**

6.  She got an MBA after graduating with a sociology degree.
    **initialism   acronym   clipped form   portmanteau**

7.  They're saving money, so this summer they just did a staycation.
    **initialism   acronym   clipped form   portmanteau**

8.  The kids play basketball every Tuesday at the rec center.
    **initialism   acronym   clipped form   portmanteau**

9.  Did you know that Moscow was founded in 1147 CE?
    **initialism   acronym   clipped form   portmanteau**

10. The USA PATRIOT Act was passed shortly after the 9/11 attacks.
    **initialism   acronym   clipped form   portmanteau**

11. Each candidate is getting support from numerous PACs.
    **initialism   acronym   clipped form   portmanteau**

12.  Superhero movies have become much more popular than rom-coms.
     **initialism   acronym   clipped form   portmanteau**

13.  Her senior film project was a docudrama about cactus hunters.
     **initialism   acronym   clipped form   portmanteau**

14.  Their French lit final involves reading passages and identifying the authors.
     **initialism   acronym   clipped form   portmanteau**

15.  They've petitioned to make that a UNESCO World Heritage Site.
     **initialism   acronym   clipped form   portmanteau**

_____

*Answers can be found on page 200.*

# 10.0

## PRONOUNS

WORDS

**P**ronouns, as mentioned in chapter 3, stand in for a noun or noun phrase. They have a few more specific uses as well, such as asking questions, showing when a noun is unknown or undetermined, pointing things out, and introducing relative clauses. The noun a pronoun stands in for is called the **antecedent**.

## 10.1 Personal Pronouns

Personal pronouns don't just refer to people: They stand in for people or things and carry with them information about first, second, or third person (see section 6.2); singular or plural number (see section 6.3); and case (see section 10.2). They have subject, object, possessive (see section 10.3), and reflexive (see section 10.5) forms.

| SINGULAR | | | | | |
|---|---|---|---|---|---|
| Person | Subject | Object | Possessive pronoun | Possessive adjective | Reflexive/ intensive |
| *First* | I | me | mine | my | myself |
| *Second* | you | you | yours | your | yourself |
| *Third* | | | | | |
| *Masculine* | he | him | his | his | himself |
| *Feminine* | she | her | hers | her | herself |
| *Neuter* | it | it | its | its | itself |
| *Gender-neutral\** | they | them | theirs | their | themselves |

| PLURAL | | | | | |
|---|---|---|---|---|---|
| Person | Subject | Object | Possessive pronoun | Possessive adjective | Reflexive/ intensive |
| *First* | we | us | ours | our | ourselves |
| *Second* | you | you | yours | your | yourselves |
| *Third* | they | them | theirs | their | themselves |

\*See section 10.1.1, singular "they."

### 10.1.1 SINGULAR "THEY"

Although *they* is traditionally plural, it's been used as a singular for centuries when the antecedent is an unknown or generic person, as in *If anyone calls, tell them I'll be back in 15 minutes*. Shakespeare used it, Jane Austen used it, even the King James Bible used it.

As singular *they* has become more accepted in the mainstream—newspapers and popular magazines use it, and even some usage guides are giving it the stamp of approval—some people still insist that a singular antecedent must always have a singular pronoun. (It's interesting that no one argues we should use only *thou* and *thee* instead of singular *you*.) But singular *they* is here because we need it, and it's staying because we use it and understand it. Singular *they* is a more inclusive choice than using *he* to refer to a generic person, and a less clunky choice than using *he or she* throughout a piece of writing.

If it happens that you are writing in a highly formal context, or for a boss or teacher who's a real stickler, the easiest way around using *they* as a singular is to use it as a plural: Instead of writing *Each new hire* must pick up *his or her ID* on the first day, just make the subject plural: *All new hires* must pick up *their IDs* on the first day. This doesn't always work, but it does the trick most of the time and keeps the sentence smooth and inclusive.

**PRACTICE EXERCISE 10.1**

## PERSONAL PRONOUNS

Circle the personal pronoun in each sentence.

1.  Oh, say can you see by the dawn's early light?

2.  One day she just up and left.

3.  I don't want to live in Alabama.

4.  If Marco doesn't get here soon, we are going to be late.

5.  Can Grandpa see them from here?

**KEY FOR PRACTICE EXERCISE 10.1**

1.  you
2.  she
3.  I
4.  we
5.  them

# 10.2 Subject and Object Pronouns

Some personal pronouns plus the pronoun *who* have different forms depending on their "case"—that is, whether they're **subjects** or **objects**. Some languages, such as German, Latin, and Russian, have multiple cases—and multiple forms—for each noun, pronoun, and adjective that show their role in the sentence. English has lost those case differences except for a handful of pronouns. Also, we're down to just subject and object forms—regardless of whether a pronoun is a direct object, an indirect object, or the object of a preposition, the object form is the same.

Trouble usually occurs in two spots: (1) when people use an object pronoun in a subject spot, such as *Me and Jake went out for coffee,* which should be *Jake and I* (word order is a convention of English but not a grammatical rule; using *I* for a subject is a grammatical rule), and (2) when people use a subject pronoun in an object spot, such as *The teacher asked Hayley and I to do the problem on the board*, which should be *Hayley and me*. The way to determine which pronoun you need is to look at the pronoun alone: <u>*Me went out for coffee*</u>? No, <u>*I went*</u>. <u>*The teacher asked I*</u> *to do the problem*? No, <u>*the teacher asked me*</u>. It's immediately clear when you take pronouns one at a time. Remember that *between* is a preposition and should always have object pronouns.

### 10.2.1 WHO AND WHOM

*Whom* is the object form of *who*, and it's slowly making an exit from English. In most informal writing, it's fine to use *who* everywhere except directly following a preposition (the "to whom it may concern" category).

However, in more formal writing you may still need to use *whom*, so use this test to determine which one you need: Swap in the pronoun *he* or *him* and see which one makes sense. If it's *he*, use *who*, and if it's *him*, use *whom* (easy to remember because both end in *m*). For example: *The new director, _____ we all think is a good leader, will arrive next month*. We all think *he* is a good leader? Yes, so *who* is the right choice.

Be careful when a *who* heads up a relative clause (see sections 5.5 and 10.6) following a preposition: It looks as if it should be an object, but it might not be. Mistakes frequently pop up in sentences such as this: *Give the envelope to <u>whomever</u> is working the front desk*. The *he/him* test still works: <u>*Him is working the front desk*</u>? No, <u>*he is working*</u>, so *whoever* is correct here.

When in doubt, use *who*—you may be wrong, but almost no one will notice, and it's better than being wrong *and* pretentious with a misplaced *whom*.

## 10.2.2 EXCEPTIONS TO SUBJECT/OBJECT DISTINCTION

With linking verbs (see section 6.7), the predicate is not an object but a complement, and so a pronoun technically should be a subject pronoun. But most US speakers, in constructions such as *It's me* or *That's her*, use the object form. The subject form is so unusual that it sounds stuffy or even incorrect, and the object form is so common that it's accepted as standard, so know that it's fine to say *It's only us*.

---

### PRACTICE EXERCISE 10.2

## SUBJECT AND OBJECT PRONOUNS

Circle the correct pronoun in each sentence.

1. The manager gave Barry and **she / her** extra work to do because I was out sick.

2. They were planning a party for his cousin and **he / him**.

3. I was startled when the doorbell rang at midnight, but relieved when it was just **they / them** on the porch.

4. The ship's captain, **who / whom** the crew said was capricious and cruel, was eager to reach the island.

5. Just between you and **I / me**, the potato salad smells a bit funny.

**KEY FOR PRACTICE EXERCISE 10.2**

1. her
2. him
3. them
4. who
5. me

## 10.3 Possessives

Personal pronouns have two possessive forms: possessive pronouns and possessive adjectives. Pronouns stand alone: *That seat is mine*. Adjectives precede a noun: *That is my seat*. Refer to the table in section 10.1 for all the personal pronoun forms.

   The most common mistake with possessive pronouns and adjectives is to add apostrophes. Although possessive nouns (see section 8.2) are formed with apostrophes, possessive pronouns aren't. If you see an apostrophe with a pronoun, it should be a contraction, so say it as two words. If the sentence doesn't make sense, then you have the wrong form. For example: *It's name is Tigger*. *It is name is Tigger*? No, so you want *its*, with no apostrophe.

---

**PRACTICE EXERCISE 10.3**

### POSSESSIVES

Circle the correct pronoun form in each sentence.

1. **You're / Your** hair looks terrific!

2. You can't take that dog—he's **ours / our's**.

3. Her uncles sold **their / they're / there** farm in Missouri.

4. Have you met that new friend of **her's / hers**?

5. I hear **its / it's** supposed to snow tonight.

**KEY FOR PRACTICE EXERCISE 10.3**
1. Your
2. ours
3. their
4. hers
5. it's (= it is)

## 10.4 Pronoun Agreement

A pronoun needs to "agree" with its antecedent in number just as a verb agrees with its subject (see section 5.2). This means that a singular noun gets a singular pronoun, and a plural noun gets a plural pronoun.

The most common trouble spot with this is when we have a singular noun that includes multiple people, such as *band, audience,* and *organization.* In British English, these nouns take plural verbs and pronouns, even though they're singular. But in US English, they take singular verbs and singular pronouns. People don't usually use a plural verb with a word such as *business* (*The business is growing*) but they often stick in a plural pronoun (*The business is expanding their product line*). This is no big deal in conversation, but when you're writing formally or professionally, stick to singular pronouns.

---

**PRACTICE EXERCISE 10.4**

### PRONOUN AGREEMENT

Circle the correct pronoun in each sentence.

1. The new restaurant is having **their / its** grand opening on Saturday.

2. Under the new curriculum, students will fulfill six requirements through **his or her / their** coursework, regardless of major.

3. The team ended **their / its** five-game losing streak on Sunday.

4. The players are rested and ready for **their / its** game tomorrow.

5. The international conglomerate is building **their / its** new executive center in the Kansas City area.

KEY FOR PRACTICE EXERCISE 10.4

1. its
2. their
3. its
4. their
5. its

## 10.5 Reflexive and Intensive Pronouns

Reflexives and intensives—the *-self/-selves* forms of personal pronouns—look exactly the same but have different functions.

**Reflexive** pronouns "reflect" back on the subject, which means that the subject of the sentence is the antecedent of the pronoun. For example: *Serena bought herself a new car*. Here, the indirect object, *herself*, and the subject, *Serena*, are the same person. By definition, reflexive pronouns cannot be used as subjects, so avoid sentences such as *Minerva and myself will present the report at the meeting* (use *Minerva and I* instead). Reflexives also should not be used as objects when the object and the subject are different, so avoid sentences such as *The teacher reprimanded Caleb and myself* (use *Caleb and me* instead).

**Intensive** pronouns emphasize the subject as the doer of the action: *I wrote the poems myself. Against stupidity, the gods themselves contend in vain.* Intensives can occur before or after the verb in the sentence.

**PRACTICE EXERCISE 10.5**

# REFLEXIVE AND INTENSIVE PRONOUNS

Circle the correct pronoun in each sentence.

1. The CEO set the deadline for the report **her / herself**.

2. When Bill and **I / me / myself** were chosen for the panel, we started working right away.

3. The children are old enough to read their bedtime stories **them / themselves**.

4. Cheri invited Aliyah and **I / me / myself** to her potluck and asked us to bring a vegetarian dish.

5. She's organizing the potluck instead of a throwing a birthday party for **her / herself**.

**KEY FOR PRACTICE EXERCISE 10.5**

1. herself (intensive)
2. I (subject)
3. themselves (reflexive)
4. me (direct object)
5. herself (reflexive)

## 10.6 Relative Pronouns

A relative clause (see section 5.4) provides more information about a noun in the main clause. It is linked to the main clause by a relative pronoun—*who/whom, which,* and *that. Who* and *whom* (see section 10.2) are preferred for people, and *which* and *that* for things, but it's not ungrammatical to use *that* with people. For example: *The Khatibs, <u>who</u> live next door to us, have a pool. The boy <u>that</u> you saw earlier is their son.* The relative pronoun can be a subject or an object in the relative clause. Here's an example where it's an object: *Adele Khan, <u>whom</u> you'll meet later today, is a potential client.*

Relative clauses can be **essential** or **nonessential**. Essential clauses are necessary for the sentence to make sense: *Throw away the pencils <u>that</u> have no erasers.* We don't want *all* the pencils thrown away, just the ones without erasers—so that piece of information is **essential** for the sentence. Nonessential clauses give "extra bonus information" about the noun. In US English, *that* is used with essential clauses and *which* is used with nonessential clauses. *Who* is used with both, and punctuation is what distinguishes them. (For punctuation guidelines, see section 16.2.) When a relative clause is essential, it's often, but not always, okay to drop the relative pronoun and sometimes even a linking verb: *The supplies (<u>that</u>) I need for this project are back-ordered. The officials (<u>who are</u>) visiting tomorrow will be inspecting the labs.*

Relative pronouns can also be **possessive**; *whose* is the only possessive form, used with both people and things. For example: *The Schumms, <u>whose</u> house is on the corner, have lived here since the neighborhood was built.* They also have **indefinite** (see section 10.9) forms—*whoever, whomever, whosever,* and *whichever*—which are used when you are uncertain or don't need to be specific. For example: *<u>Whoever</u> spilled coffee all over the break room should clean it up. That car alarm, <u>whosever</u> it is, is really annoying.* (Yes, *whosever* is a real word.)

**PRACTICE EXERCISE 10.6**

## RELATIVE PRONOUNS

Circle the relative pronoun in each sentence.

1. The students who did their homework all did well on the quiz.

2. The parcel, which was left on the front steps, got soaked during the rainstorm.

3. Carol, whose paintings are on display at the coffee shop, is a talented watercolorist.

4. The team that has the most points across categories wins the competition.

5. This cupboard has whichever folder you need.

**KEY FOR PRACTICE EXERCISE 10.6**

1. who
2. which
3. whose
4. that
5. whichever

## 10.7 Demonstratives

Demonstratives point things out and can contrast things or note whether they are close by or farther away. Like possessives (see section 10.3), demonstratives can work as pronouns (standing alone) or as adjectives (preceding a noun). The demonstratives are *this, that, these,* and *those.*

*This* and *these* usually refer to whatever is closer, in physical distance, figurative distance, or time. *This is the book I was talking about. These plates are going in the garage sale; those are staying. That* and *those* are usually used with something more distant (again, literally, figuratively, or temporally): *That house down the street has been on the market for ages*. Sometimes the distinction is extremely fine: *I can't read type of this size* would likely imply you're looking right at the document; *I can't read type of that size* may be trying to convey the reason you haven't read it.

---

**PRACTICE EXERCISE 10.7**

## DEMONSTRATIVES

In each sentence, identify whether the demonstrative is a pronoun or an adjective.

1. That's how we roll.
   **pronoun   adjective**

2. This code opens the main door.
   **pronoun   adjective**

3. This is my roommate, Sheldon.
   **pronoun   adjective**

4. Those people are acting strangely.
   **pronoun   adjective**

5. Don't worry about that.
   **pronoun   adjective**

---

**KEY FOR PRACTICE EXERCISE 10.7**

1. pronoun
2. adjective
3. pronoun
4. adjective
5. pronoun

## 10.8 Interrogative Pronouns

Interrogative pronouns are used to ask questions whose answer is a noun: Who? What? Which? Whom? Whose? Even when a pronoun is an object in the sentence, it comes first in a question: *What did you see out the window? Who was in the parking lot? Whose car was it?* Sometimes these work like adjectives (see Chapter 12) because they are paired with a noun: *Which car got stolen?* Even when an interrogative is an object in the sentence, it comes first in a question. *Whom did the police interview about it?*

### PRACTICE EXERCISE 10.8

### INTERROGATIVE PRONOUNS

Circle the correct interrogative in each sentence.

1. **Who / Whom / What** threw away those papers?

2. **Which / Whose / What** do you want for dinner tonight?

3. **What / Which / Whose** time do we need to leave for the seminar?

4. **Who / Whom / Whose** backpack is that?

5. **Which / Who / Whom** calendar should I put the meeting on?

### KEY FOR PRACTICE EXERCISE 10.8

1. Who
2. What
3. What
4. Whose
5. Which

## 10.9 Indefinite Pronouns

Indefinite pronouns, as the name suggests, do not refer to anything definite—that is, they don't have a specific antecedent. They can indicate a nonspecific quantity (*few, some, many, much,* etc.) or a general or unspecified thing or person (*someone, anything, anybody,* etc.), or include or exclude members of a set (*all, none, either, each, neither, both,* etc.).

The main area of trouble with indefinite pronouns is number: Are they singular or plural? In fact, some are singular (*anyone, everybody, something, each, either, one,* etc.), some are plural (*both, few, several, many*), and some can be both. The "can be both" ones are *all, any, more, most, none,* and *some.* Whether they're singular or plural depends on what sort of thing they refer to: If it's singular, use a singular verb; if it's plural, use a plural verb. For example: *All the paint is gone.* Here, *paint* is singular, so use *is.* But: *All the cookies are gone. Cookies* is plural, so use *are.* Same with *none*—grammar books once stated that *none* must always be singular, but it depends. For example: *None of the gluten-free, vegan pizza was eaten.* One pizza, singular. But: *None of the gluten-free, vegan pizzas were eaten.* Multiple pizzas, plural.

---

**PRACTICE EXERCISE 10.9**

### INDEFINITE PRONOUNS

Circle the correct verb in each sentence. (Don't overthink it—what "sounds right" probably is.)

1. Before we go out, let's make sure our homework **is / are** done.

2. The square root of nine? Everybody **knows / know** that!

3. Some of our friends **is / are** part of that club.

4. **Does / Do** anyone know the way to Hudson Bay?

5. Both of the hallways **leads / lead** to the main auditorium.

*(continued)*

(continued)

**KEY FOR PRACTICE EXERCISE 10.9**

1. is
2. knows
3. are
4. Does
5. lead

## 10.10 Dummy Subjects

Another use of pronouns is as "dummy subjects," which is when you have a pronoun working grammatically as the subject of a sentence—such as *It is, It appears, There is/are,* and *This is*—but it's a placeholder instead of the main information of the sentence.

Dummy subjects are grammatical, and sometimes even required, as in weather expressions like *It's raining* or *It's supposed to snow tomorrow*, but often they're overly wordy and add an unnecessary complexity to a sentence. Sometimes they're a sign of a vague passive-voice sentence (see section 6.6). Dummy subjects delay the real subject, shifting information away from the front of a sentence. This shift isn't always bad, but in most cases, starting with the true subject makes a clearer, more concise sentence. For example, *There were thousands of screaming fans packing the arena* would be stronger as *Thousands of screaming fans packed the arena*. Notice that the verb may need an adjustment when you take out a dummy subject, usually turning a participle into a true verb (here, *packing* into *packed*).

Use *there is* when the complement is singular and *there are* when it's plural: *There is no reason for you to be afraid. There are several typos on this menu.*

But sometimes a dummy subject is the best choice: Perhaps a transition is smoother with one, or a demonstrative shows emphasis, or rhetorically a dummy subject is more effective. Who among us would rewrite Austen's "It is a truth universally acknowledged" or Dickens's "It was the best of times, it was the worst of times"?

## PRACTICE EXERCISE 10.10

# DUMMY SUBJECTS

Rewrite each sentence without using a dummy subject.

1. It is Venice where they want to go on their honeymoon.

2. There was one factor that was ignored by proponents of the plan, and that was unintended water contamination.

3. After the storm, there were a number of houses and businesses that reported damage.

4. It is suggested on the writing website that writers should avoid using dummy subjects.

5. It is the consensus of experts that direct, concise sentences are easier to understand.

### KEY FOR PRACTICE EXERCISE 10.10

1. They want to go to Venice on their honeymoon.
2. One factor was ignored by proponents of the plan: unintended water contamination.
3. After the storm, a number of houses and businesses reported damage.
4. The writing website suggests that writers should avoid using dummy subjects.
5. Experts agree that direct, concise sentences are easier to understand.

## QUIZ FOR CHAPTER 10: PRONOUNS

For questions 1–18, circle the correct answer.

1. **Whose / Who's / Whom's** new phone is that?

2. I like to think I judge a book by **its / it's** content instead of **its / it's** cover.

3. Susan and **I / me** made dessert.

4. We know **they / them** won first place, but we think we did better.

5. Please hand your ticket to John or **I / me** when you are ready to go in.

6. We plan to vote for the politician **who / whom** best represents our interests.

7. The director is the person to **who / whom** Laura was referring.

8. Give it to the person **who / whom** needs it the most.

9. Be sure to tell Nicola or **I / me** where we're meeting Saturday.

10. The jazz band and the dance ensemble had **its / their** annual joint concert last weekend.

11. **Does / Do** anyone need to use the restroom?

12. After the merger, the company moved **its / their** headquarters out of state.

13. Both of her sisters **lives / live** in Chicago.

14. **Who / Whom** is going to the poetry reading tonight?

15. Did you remember **your / you're** passport?

16. The tour group told Rachel and **I / me / myself** all about the flight delay.

17. Everyone in the group **was / were** exhausted and just wanted to sleep.

18. Sam and **I / me / myself** have solos in the upcoming performance.

For questions 19–25, match the pronoun with its category. (Some might match with more than one category!)

| | | |
|---|---|---|
| 19. | he | **possessive** |
| 20. | themselves | **interrogative** |
| 21. | who | **personal** |
| 22. | that | **indefinite** |
| 23. | anyone | **relative** |
| 24. | what | **demonstrative** |
| 25. | your | **reflexive** |

*Answers can be found on page 201.*

# 11.0
## ADJECTIVES

WORDS

A djectives describe, or modify, a noun, and usually answer the question "what kind?" or "which one?" Adjectives usually come before a noun, as in a *pretty* sunset. But they can be part of a predicate with a linking verb, as in *The sunset is pretty*, or even come after a noun: *We saw a sunset pretty as can be*. Adjectives themselves can be modified by adverbs (see chapter 12), as in *surprisingly pretty*.

## 11.1 Order of Adjectives

Nouns can have more than one adjective modifying them, and there's a certain order the adjectives will usually occur in the sentence. Native English speakers will have no problem with this: A sentence just "sounds weird" if the adjectives are out of place. But if you aren't a native speaker, or are just curious, here is the order for English (it varies by language):

1. Number (either a specific number or an indefinite quantifier like "some")
2. Quality, value, or opinion (good, bad, ugly, delicious, cheap, etc.)
3. Size (literally or figuratively—big, small, etc.)
4. Temperature (literally or figuratively—hot, cold, etc.)
5. Age (old, new, etc.)
6. Shape (round, square, pear-shaped, etc.)
7. Color (blue, green, etc.)
8. Origin (can be a country/region or time period)
9. Material (wooden, cloth, stone, etc.)

So we would have *four Amish wooden chairs*, or *sturdy big white chairs*, or *four sturdy big white Amish wooden chairs*. If the noun happens to be a compound, like "dining chairs," the compounding adjective is closest to the noun: *four sturdy big white Amish wooden dining chairs*.

Not surprisingly, you will occasionally come across exceptions to this order, such as *big bad wolf*. See section 16.4.5 for guidelines on when to use commas to separate lists of adjectives, as in *a friendly, welcoming place* and *a frustrating, exhausting day*.

**PRACTICE EXERCISE 11.1**

## ORDER OF ADJECTIVES

Rewrite each phrase with the list of adjectives in the correct order.

1. **new / black / expensive** dress

2. **green / little / several** aliens

3. **stinking / hot / big** mess

4. **Russian / colorful / wooden** toy

5. **fluffy / three / white** kittens

**KEY FOR PRACTICE EXERCISE 11.1**

1. expensive new black dress

2. several little green aliens

3. big hot stinking mess

4. colorful Russian wooden toy

5. three fluffy white kittens

## 11.2 Comparatives and Superlatives

**Comparative** adjectives are used to compare two nouns: *He is bigger, faster, and stronger than his brother, but his brother is more handsome and more sophisticated*. Use comparatives only when you have two people or two things to compare. Comparatives are formed in one of two ways: By adding *-er* or by putting *more* in front of the adjective. Generally, short words become comparative with *-er* and longer ones with *more*, but, because this is English, there are lots of exceptions, and some words use both formations: For example, you've probably run into both *stupider* and *more stupid*.

**Superlative** adjectives are used to show the "most adjective" item in a group. These are the best, worst, biggest, smallest, "most" whatever noun you have. The group can be small: *Of their three daughters, Betty is the <u>oldest</u>.* Or it can be large: *They built the <u>most expensive</u> hotel in the world.* Superlatives are formed in a similar way to comparatives: by adding *-est* or by putting *most* in front of the adjective.

Some adjectives, including the common ones *good, bad, far, little,* and *much,* have irregular comparatives and superlatives (*good / better / best* and so on). Most dictionaries give the comparative and superlative forms, so when in doubt, look it up.

---

**PRACTICE EXERCISE 11.2**

## COMPARATIVES AND SUPERLATIVES

Fill in the comparative and superlative forms of each adjective.
Use a dictionary if you need to.

| Adjective | Comparative | Superlative |
|---|---|---|
| 1. fuzzy | _____ | _____ |
| 2. blue | _____ | _____ |
| 3. ancient | _____ | _____ |
| 4. bad | _____ | _____ |
| 5. eminent | _____ | _____ |

*(continued)*

*(continued)*

**KEY FOR PRACTICE EXERCISE 11.2**

1.  fuzzy, fuzzier, fuzziest
2.  blue, bluer, bluest
3.  ancient, more ancient, most ancient
4.  bad, worse, worst
5.  eminent, more eminent, most eminent

## 11.3 Proper Adjectives

When proper nouns (see section 8.7) get an adjective form or are themselves used as adjectives, the result is **proper adjectives**: _French_ literature, _Texas_ toast, a _Herculean_ task, a _Kafkaesque_ experience. Just like proper nouns, these are capitalized.

## 11.4 Compound Adjectives

We saw above how adjectives can stack up in a particular order, but sometimes two or more words combine to form a **compound adjective** that expresses a single descriptive concept, such as _life-threatening_ injuries or _stand-up_ comedy. Compound adjectives are often hyphenated (for more on hyphens, see section 16.2.1), except for adjective-adverb combinations where the adverb ends in -_ly_: a _poorly timed_ announcement; _barely audible_ instructions. Pairings with most adverbs that don't end in -_ly_ do take a hyphen: a _well-known_ author; _a much-anticipated renovation_.

Longer phrases or common expressions used as adjectives sometimes appear in quotation marks instead of being hyphenated: a _"light bulb"_ moment, a _"punch in the gut"_ piece of news.

**PRACTICE EXERCISE 11.4**

# COMPOUND ADJECTIVES

Change each phrase into a compound adjective.

1.  an opportunity that comes once in a lifetime →
    a _____ opportunity

2.  negotiations at a high level →
    _____ negotiations

3.  the owner of a small business →
    the _____ owner

4.  skills in speech writing →
    _____ skills

5.  a signal from ship to shore →
    a _____ signal

**KEY FOR PRACTICE EXERCISE 11.4**

1.  a once-in-a-lifetime opportunity
2.  high-level negotiations
3.  the small-business owner
4.  speech-writing skills
5.  a ship-to-shore signal

## 11.5 Indefinite Adjectives

**Indefinite adjectives**, similar to indefinite pronouns (see section 10.9), modify a noun to indicate a nonspecific quantity (*few, some, several, many,* etc.) or to include or exclude members of a set (*all, any, each, every, no, both,* etc.). The difference between indefinite pronouns and indefinite adjectives—the same word is often used for both—is that the pronouns stand alone and the adjectives come before a noun: <u>*some*</u> *say* (pronoun) versus <u>*some*</u> *people say* (adjective).

## 11.6 Intensifiers

Some adverbs (see chapter 12), called **intensifiers**—words such as *really, very, pretty, fairly, quite,* and so on—indicate how much of an adjective's quality the noun has. Intensifiers are common in speech but should be used sparingly in writing because without verbal and visual cues from a speaker, they're often so vague they are meaningless. The famous newspaper editor William Allen White had a directive in the style guide for his paper, the *Emporia Gazette*: "Very: If you must use this word, the Boss says to make it read 'damn.' Then the copy editor will be sure to spot it and kill it."

If you find yourself writing with intensifiers, stop and think about whether you could use a stronger adjective instead: *Really big*? How about *huge*? *Very tasty*? How about *delicious*? You won't always be able to do it, but even doing it some of the time will make your writing clearer and more interesting.

# INTENSIFIERS

Match each intensifier + adjective with the single adjective that shares its meaning.

| | | |
|---|---|---|
| 1. | a *rather pretty* bracelet | soaked |
| 2. | an *extremely small* chance | lovely |
| 3. | a *pretty ordinary* film | thunderous |
| 4. | *really wet* shoes | mediocre |
| 5. | a *very loud* crowd | minuscule |

**KEY FOR PRACTICE EXERCISE 11.6**

1. rather pretty / lovely
2. extremely small / minuscule
3. pretty ordinary / mediocre
4. really wet / soaked
5. very loud / thunderous

## QUIZ FOR CHAPTER 11: ADJECTIVES

For questions 1–8, number the adjectives according to their order.

**At the bazaar, she bought . . . scarves.**

1.    ___ French

2.    ___ little

3.    ___ triangular

4.    ___ two

5.    ___ silk

6.    ___ old

7.    ___ green

8.    ___ gorgeous

For questions 9–15, form an appropriate comparative or superlative from the underlined adjective.

9.    Darren is <u>fast</u>, but he's not the _____ runner on the squad.

10.    Natasha looks <u>young</u> for her age, but her sister looks _____.

11.    They told us it wasn't that <u>far</u> off the road, but it's _____ than we thought.

12.    Nick is <u>smart</u>; in fact, he's one of the _____ people I know.

13.    This meeting is <u>important</u>, but the call I have to take is _____.

14.    She loves Key West because it's so <u>peaceful</u>. She says it's the
_____ place she's visited.

15.    The hummus here is <u>good</u>, but the baba ghanoush is even
_____.

For questions 16–20, identify what kind of adjective the underlined word is.

16.    The team got involved in a <u>no-holds-barred</u> barroom brawl.
       **comparative  superlative  proper  compound  indefinite**

17.    Their <u>younger</u> daughter, Jessica, is starting a graduate program.
       **comparative  superlative  proper  compound  indefinite**

18.    The <u>German</u> chocolate cake was the first one gone.
       **comparative  superlative  proper  compound  indefinite**

19.    <u>Any</u> coat left in the library will be turned in to the main office.
       **comparative  superlative  proper  compound  indefinite**

20.    This year's race raised the <u>most</u> money ever.
       **comparative  superlative  proper  compound  indefinite**

_____

*Answers can be found on page 201.*

# 12.0
## ADVERBS

WORDS

**A**dverbs, as introduced in chapter 3, modify verbs, adjectives, or other adverbs, usually answering questions of time ("when?"), location ("where?"), manner ("how?"), or degree or quality ("how much?")

*I put the groceries <u>there</u>.* (location)

*Let's leave <u>soon</u>.* (time)

*We drove <u>carefully</u> down the icy road.* (manner)

*Her designs are <u>stunningly</u> beautiful.* (degree)

Adverbs are often formed by adding -ly to an adjective, such as *quickly* and *beautifully*, but not all adverbs end in -ly (such as *well*) and not all words ending in -ly are adverbs (for example, *costly, deadly,* and *neighborly* are all adjectives). Some words have the same forms for adjectives and adverbs, such as *fast*, *hard,* and *early.* Occasionally an adjective generates two adverb forms with different meanings—for instance, *right* gives us both *right* (as in correctly: *Make sure you spell her name <u>right</u>*) and *rightly* (as in properly or appropriately: *He <u>rightly</u> brought up that we couldn't vote without a quorum*).

Like adjectives (see section 11.2), adverbs can have **comparative** and **superlative** forms: *Harry speaks Chinese <u>more fluently</u> than we expected. Claudia plays the piano <u>better</u> than her brother does. The colors in Jo's painting shone <u>the most brightly</u>.* The vast majority of comparative and superlative adverbs are formed with "more" and "most," though some common ones (such as *better/best* and *worse/worst*) have specific forms.

A piece of advice often given in writing guides is to avoid adverbs or strictly limit them. Adverbs are perfectly grammatical and necessary in writing, but be careful about overusing adverbs or using an adverb plus a verb or an adjective when a stronger verb or adjective would be better (see section 11.6).

## 12.1 Conjunctive Adverbs

This type of adverb helps provide a transition between two ideas. It can start a sentence or join a phrase or a clause to a sentence: *The summer has been extremely dry. Consequently, we've had very few mosquitoes.* Common conjunctive adverbs are *therefore, however, moreover, nevertheless, likewise, thus,* and *also.*

If a conjunctive adverb comes in the middle of a sentence joining two clauses, it's usually preceded by a semicolon and followed by a comma: *She said she wanted to study in Prague; indeed, she's going in the spring. We wanted to change the timeline of the project; however, we were overruled.*

## 12.2 Sentence Adverbs

Some adverbs come at the beginning of a sentence and modify the whole sentence: *Generally, we place completed requisition forms in this box. Frankly, my dear, I don't give a damn. Seriously, did no one reorder printer toner?* They are usually followed by a comma.

Modifying a sentence is a legitimate use of adverbs. You should know, though, that there's a long-standing peeve about the adverb "hopefully" being used as a sentence adverb meaning *I hope* or *we hope* (instead of *in a hopeful manner*, despite the fact that the *I hope* sense is several centuries old). For decades, usage manuals and style guides advised against *hopefully* as a sentence adverb (the *Associated Press Stylebook* lifted its prohibition on this use of *hopefully* only in 2012). Be aware that many people—some of whom will be reading and evaluating your writing—still have it in their heads that a sentence with *hopefully* is wrong, even though it's not, so think about your audience before you use it.

# QUIZ FOR CHAPTER 12: ADVERBS

Circle the adverb in the sentence and then indicate what type of adverb it is.

1.  Bob passionately collects Harley-Davidson memorabilia.
    **time location manner degree conjunctive sentence**

2.  The zombies furiously attacked the abandoned airport.
    **time location manner degree conjunctive sentence**

3.  Though written well, the essay was riddled with factual errors.
    **time location manner degree conjunctive sentence**

4.  Alex gave an excellent answer in class yesterday.
    **time location manner degree conjunctive sentence**

5.  You should be extremely careful when handling fireworks.
    **time location manner degree conjunctive sentence**

6.  Apparently, they left because their son was sick.
    **time location manner degree conjunctive sentence**

7.  Matthew rejected the revisions. Nevertheless, the journal will publish his report.
    **time location manner degree conjunctive sentence**

8.  If we want to make it to the game on time, we need to leave now.
    **time location manner degree conjunctive sentence**

9.  We have three deadlines this week; moreover, top management is visiting.
    **time location manner degree conjunctive sentence**

10. Fiona is not in her office—she went out.
    **time location manner degree conjunctive sentence**

---

*Answers can be found on page 202.*

# 13.0
## PREPOSITIONS

WORDS

A s introduced in chapter 3, **prepositions** connect nouns to other information in the sentence. Prepositions always have an object (see section 5.3), which is the noun or pronoun the preposition connects to something else in the sentence.

Prepositional phrases can function like adjectives (see chapter 11), describing a noun and answering the question "which one?" or "what kind?" They can also function like adverbs (see chapter 12), modifying a verb, adjective, or other adverb and giving more information about time, place, manner, or degree.

Common prepositions include *in, out, on, off, with, about, between, beside, along, before, after, at, among, for, to, from, up, down, above, below, under,* and *over*. Many words that are prepositions are also adverbs, so look for an object to see whether a word is a true preposition.

## QUIZ FOR CHAPTER 13: PREPOSITIONS

Circle the preposition in each sentence and then indicate whether
the prepositional phrase functions like an adjective or adverb.

1.    Greta went out the door and met the mail carrier.
      **adjective    adverb**

2.    The building on the corner burned down.
      **adjective    adverb**

3.    The message from the kidnappers was untraceable.
      **adjective    adverb**

4.    The defensive linemen were all sore from yesterday's practice.
      **adjective    adverb**

5.    Summoning his courage, Homer ate a ghost chili pepper at the county fair.
      **adjective    adverb**

6.    Stacey is reading a book about the London sewers.
      **adjective    adverb**

7.    Employees are supposed to wash their hands after clearing tables.
      **adjective    adverb**

8.    That hotel is more expensive because it is on the beach.
      **adjective    adverb**

9.    Even if we drive all day, we won't make it there before nightfall.
      **adjective    adverb**

10.   She liked the house with the finished basement better than the others.
      **adjective    adverb**

_Answers can be found on page 202._

# 14.0
## CONJUNCTIONS

WORDS

I f you've ever seen the *Schoolhouse Rock!* cartoon about conjunctions, you'll know that they're for "hooking up words and phrases and clauses." (If you haven't seen it, it's on the Internet—earworm warning.) Conjunctions link elements of a sentence, and they can do this in several ways.

## 14.1 Coordinating Conjunctions

**Coordinating** conjunctions are the most common kind of conjunction. They simply join two or more similar elements of a sentence: words, phrases, or clauses.

> *We bought tomatoes, squash, and zucchini at the market.* (words are joined)
>
> *The twins ran out the door and down the street.* (phrases are joined)
>
> *Lift the cover but don't press the red button.* (clauses are joined)

Remember the coordinating conjunctions with the acronym FANBOYS: *for, and, nor, but, or, yet, so.*

## 14.2 Correlative Conjunctions

**Correlative** conjunctions come in pairs: *both . . . and, either . . . or, neither . . . nor, not . . . but, not only . . . but also,* and *whether . . . or.* The important thing to remember with correlative conjunctions is that the structure of the linked elements must be parallel (see section 5.9). For example, if one of the pair introduces a prepositional phrase, the other should too: *Max and Muffin left muddy paw prints not only on the kitchen floor but also in the dining room.*

## 14.3 Subordinating Conjunctions

**Subordinating** conjunctions go at the beginning of a clause—in the process creating a subordinate clause—and link that subordinate clause to another clause (see section 5.5). Often, subordinating conjunctions help explain time sequence, actions, results, and *if/then* conditional situations.

*Now that you're here, can you help with dinner?* (time)

*Because we burnt the lasagna, we ordered pizza.* (result)

*I can bring a dessert if someone else brings a salad.* (conditional)

Common subordinating conjunctions include *before, after, as, if, even if, now that, once, although, though, as long as, unless, until, when, where,* and *while*.

Some subordinating conjunctions, often ones having to do with time and place, can have adverbs modify them: *Just before your email came, I was thinking of calling you. She used to live right where the tornado hit.*

## QUIZ FOR CHAPTER 14: CONJUNCTIONS

Circle the conjunction in each sentence, then indicate what type of conjunction it is.

1. Bill gets annoyed whenever Sheila plays Nickelback songs.
   **coordinating   correlative   subordinating**

2. *The Hardy Boys* and *Nancy Drew* books are children's classics.
   **coordinating   correlative   subordinating**

3. Both the students and the faculty agreed that the policy had to change.
   **coordinating   correlative   subordinating**

4. Do you want to study for your chemistry test or history quiz first?
   **coordinating   correlative   subordinating**

5. He was astounded that Phish could not only improvise for 20 minutes but also make it interesting.
   **coordinating   correlative   subordinating**

6. She decided to continue the relationship even though he watched *Real Housewives* a bit too much for her taste.
   **coordinating   correlative   subordinating**

7. Wherever I go in the summer, I always get bug bites.
   **coordinating   correlative   subordinating**

8. Neither rain nor snow interrupts mail delivery by the US Postal Service.
   **coordinating   correlative   subordinating**

9. "The cat can stay," he said, "but I'm going."
   **coordinating   correlative   subordinating**

10. She gave me instructions to complete the assignment, so I followed them.
    **coordinating   correlative   subordinating**

*Answers can be found on page 202.*

# 15.0

## INTERJECTIONS

WORDS

As mentioned in chapter 3, **interjections** are outbursts that indicate strong emotion—joy, anger, surprise, disappointment, and so on—or give a warning, such as *Stop!* They're also used to get someone's attention, as in *Hey!*

Interjections can stand alone or be part of a sentence. If it requires an exclamation point or can be replaced by text abbreviations (such as *lol* or *OMG*) or emoji, you may have an interjection.

## QUIZ FOR CHAPTER 15: INTERJECTIONS

Circle the interjection in each sentence.

1.  Wow! This food is really spicy.

2.  Yikes, that was too close for comfort.

3.  They tried to enter the studio but she said, "Whoa, you can't go in there!"

4.  She saw the damage to her car and thought, "Oh, no, I can't afford this."

5.  I was walking down the street and then blam! The tree fell onto a delivery truck.

6.  You're going to Paris? Awesome!

7.  Holy cow, that storm last night was bad.

8.  Wait! You have to turn it on first.

9.  The quiz is postponed—yay!

10. We've had so much rain that my yard is full of mushrooms, yuck.

_Answers can be found on page 203._

# 16.0
## PUNCTUATION

PUNCTUATION

P unctuation marks are like road signs: They show readers where to go as they're reading. If punctuation is missing or wrong, readers can get lost.

## 16.1 End-of-Sentence Punctuation

**Periods (.)**, **question marks (?),** and **exclamation points (!)** are how we end sentences. Most people don't have much trouble with these, but two stylistic points should be noted.

After a period, put one space before the next sentence. The standard used to be two spaces, back when everyone used manual typewriters and computer typesetting didn't exist. Now, computers automatically adjust the spacing so we don't need to type two spaces anymore.

Avoid exclamation points in formal writing: essays, reports, research papers, proposals, executive summaries, and so on. You may need to use exclamation points in electronic communication—even professional electronic communication—so as not to look mad or curt, but when you do, use only one and make sure it's appropriate.

---

**PRACTICE EXERCISE 16.1**

### END-OF-SENTENCE PUNCTUATION

Add the appropriate punctuation mark at the end of each sentence.

1. What are you doing tonight

2. The sale starts at midnight

3. That foul ball is going to hit us—duck

4. Maybe Rodriguez w ill autograph it for you after the game

5. Do you think I should ask him

*(continued)*

---

*(continued)*

**KEY FOR PRACTICE EXERCISE 16.1**

1.   ? (question mark)
2.   . *(period)*
3.   ! *(exclamation point)*
4.   . *(period)*
5.   ? *(question mark)*

# 16.2 Joining Punctuation

**Hyphens** and **apostrophes** are two punctuation marks that join words.

### 16.2.1 HYPHENS

Hyphens join compound adjectives (see section 11.4) and are sometimes used with prefixes and suffixes. Some people love hyphens for their clarity; others think they clutter up a piece of writing. Reasonable people can disagree on this point, so it's always good to check your dictionary and stylebook to see what they say.

Hyphens can distinguish constructions such as *heavy equipment operator* (an equipment operator who is heavy) and *heavy-equipment operator* (an operator of heavy equipment), and *30-odd professors* (around 30 professors) and *30 odd professors* (a convocation of eccentric educators).

A good guideline for whether to hyphenate a compound adjective is to hyphenate if the modifying words are different parts of speech: *mixed-up world, frost-free refrigerator, sit-in protest, grass-fed cattle*. If each word modifies the next, or if two words are so commonly used together that they act as one, no hyphen is necessary: *oddly shaped room, hot dog bun, high school musical*. Let clarity be your ultimate guide. And be consistent.

Use **suspensive hyphenation** when you want to get rid of a word to tighten up a sentence with two repetitive hyphenated constructions. You can drop the first instance of the repeated word but leave the hyphen: *InterCall is a global <u>voice- and video-conferencing</u> operation.*

## 16.2.2 APOSTROPHES

Probably the most commonly misused piece of punctuation, the apostrophe has clear rules governing its use:

- Apostrophes are used for possessive nouns (see section 8.2): *the <u>cat's</u> meow, the <u>book's</u> title, <u>Margaret's</u> laptop.*
- Apostrophes are used for contractions (see section 4.4): *<u>it's</u> raining, <u>you're wet</u>, <u>don't</u> go.*
- Apostrophes *are* not used for possessive pronouns (see sections 4.5 and 10.3): *your book, their house, its place.*
- Apostrophes are *not* used for plural nouns: *tacos, professors, moms.*

Expressions such as *two <u>weeks'</u> notice* and *three <u>years'</u> experience* are typically plural possessives and take an apostrophe. Think about them as *notice of two weeks* and *experience of three years*. The *of* lets you know it's possessive and needs an apostrophe.

---

**PRACTICE EXERCISE 16.2**

## JOINING PUNCTUATION

Choose the sentence that is properly punctuated.

1. a. That building's foundation is concrete.
   b. That buildings foundation is concrete.
   c. That buildings' foundation is concrete.

2. a. It's about time you got here.
   b. Its about time you got here.

*(continued)*

*(continued)*

3.  a.  The two restaurants parking spaces should be divided evenly between them.
    b.  The two restaurant's parking spaces should be divided evenly between them.
    c.  The two restaurants' parking spaces should be divided evenly between them.

4.  a.  We were ready to leave on a seven-day road trip, then the tornado siren blared.
    b.  We were ready to leave on a seven day road trip, then the tornado siren blared.

5.  a.  The coalition knew a hearts and minds campaign was key to success.
    b.  The coalition knew a hearts- and minds-campaign was key to success.
    c.  The coalition knew a hearts-and-minds campaign was key to success.

**KEY FOR PRACTICE EXERCISE 16.2**

1.  a
2.  a
3.  c
4.  a
5.  c

## 16.3 Dividing Punctuation

Colons, semicolons, dashes, parentheses, and quotation marks all serve to set off some part of a sentence.

### 16.3.1 COLONS

A **colon (:)** signals a major break in a sentence and is used to introduce a list, an explanation or elaboration, or examples, as in *She sang about her favorite things: raindrops, roses, kitten whiskers, and death metal.* Material after a colon may be either a complete sentence or a fragment. Formal letter salutations end with a colon (*To the Editors:*).

### 16.3.2 SEMICOLONS

A **semicolon (;)** separates two independent but related clauses and elegantly avoids a comma splice (see section 16.4.8): *Curt works at Macy's; Katy works at Nordstrom.* If you have a conjunction, you don't need a semicolon: *Curt works at Macy's, <u>and</u> Katy works at Nordstrom.* The test to see whether you can use a semicolon is to put a period in the same location. If both sentences can stand alone, you can use a semicolon.

Semicolons come before a conjunctive adverb (see section 12.1) that falls in the middle of a sentence: *She wanted to plant a garden; <u>in fact</u>, she's already dug up a spot in the yard. The governor vetoed the bill; <u>moreover</u>, she warned lawmakers such a law would have been unconstitutional.*

Semicolons are also used for separating elements of a list that themselves contain commas, so readers clearly see where a new element begins: *All she brought on the plane was a granola bar; a tablet loaded with her favorite games, music, and apps; and her earbuds.*

### 16.3.3 DASHES

Use a **dash (—)** to set off descriptive material or a comment or aside within a sentence. Dashes are particularly useful if that extra material contains commas of its own or needs more separation: *My entire family—Mom, Dad, Jonah, and Liz—came to watch my spelling bee.* Dashes can also signify a sudden turn in the sentence, or a special emphasis on something at the end: *He'd never seen footprints like this—seven distinct toes.* Be mindful not to overuse dashes. Many times commas will do to set off a short phrase or a single word.

Whether to use spaces on either side of a dash is a matter for your style guide, but dashes are wider than hyphens, so don't use a hyphen when you need a dash.

### 16.3.4 PARENTHESES

Use **parentheses (())** to set off a tangential piece of information or opinion within a sentence. Parentheses are best used with a less important fact or a side comment. Parentheses are also used for citations in some style guides.

### 16.3.5 QUOTATION MARKS

Quotation marks set off word-for-word quoted material, and they should not be used simply to indicate emphasis. If you're using quoted material, use more than one word, or paraphrase, to avoid looking snarky or doubtful with "scare" quotes.

Style guides vary, but generally in US English, commas and periods go inside quotation marks, and colons and semicolons go outside. Question marks and exclamation points go inside quotation marks if they're part of the quoted material and outside if they're not.

---

**PRACTICE EXERCISE 16.3**

## DIVIDING PUNCTUATION

In each sentence, write in the appropriate dividing punctuation mark.

1. Whoever takes over the department ___ whether it's Mariel, Joe, or Aisha ___ has a big job.

2. Only one thing is required ___ a sense of humor.

3. She referred to Mencken's observation, ___ Love is like war: easy to begin but very hard to stop. ___

4. He said he liked the exhibit ___ Matisse and Van Gogh are his favorite painters.

5. The restaurant that just opened ___ my neighbor was the owner ___ is closed already.

**KEY FOR PRACTICE EXERCISE 16.3**

1. dashes
2. colon
3. quotation marks
4. semicolon
5. parentheses

## 16.4 All about Commas

Commas signal a pause or a dividing line in writing. Problems arise because there are places you must have a comma, places you shouldn't have a comma, and places where it's your choice. Follow these guidelines, but let clarity be your ultimate guide.

### 16.4.1 DIRECT ADDRESS

The comma of direct address makes the difference between *Let's eat, people!* and *Let's eat people!* Use a comma to set off a person or group being directly spoken to: one after if the address leads off the sentence, one before if the addressee is at the end, and one on either side in the middle: *Peter, did you get the memo? I've done all my chores, Mom. No, Dan, we were bowling partners.*

### 16.4.2 APPOSITIVES

Appositives are phrases that provide a little extra information about a noun. They are set off with commas before and after: *Freddy, my college roommate, is having a party next month.* Don't forget the "after" comma—that's a common mistake. Dates and places fall into this category: *On January 10, 2013, they all went to Moscow, Idaho, for a family reunion.*

### 16.4.3 NONESSENTIAL CLAUSES

These are "who" or "which" clauses (see sections 5.4 and 10.6) that, like appositives, give extra information but are not essential to the sentence. They are set off with commas before and after: *The team, which made it to the tournament in 2012, last won a championship in 2008.*

### 16.4.4 LISTS

Commas are used to separate items in a list: *The diner's specialty is a breakfast of green eggs, ham, and hash browns.* The comma after the second-to-last item (before the conjunction) is called the **serial comma** or the **Oxford comma**. Most styles in US English call for the serial comma, although Associated Press (AP) style, which is widely used by news media, says to omit it when it's not needed for clarity.

### 16.4.5 MULTIPLE ADJECTIVES

Some adjectives need to be separated by a comma and some don't. Here's how to tell: If you can reverse the order of two adjectives and the sentence still makes sense, put a comma between them: *His incompetent, cruel boss made him work Saturdays. His cruel, incompetent boss made him work Saturdays.* Both sentences make sense, so put a comma between the adjectives. If you can't switch them, no comma: *They work in a big gray building downtown. Gray big* doesn't work, so no comma should be used (for more on order of adjectives, see section 11.1).

### 16.4.6 LEAD-INS

Sentences sometimes start with a phrase or clause that leads into the main clause. Usually these lead-ins need a comma to separate them from the main clause: _Being a top pick for the team, he tried not to let the attention go to his head_. Read it out loud, and if you pause, put a comma in.

### 16.4.7 CONJUNCTIONS

Use a comma after a coordinating conjunction (see section 14.1) if both verbs have a subject: _We love hyphens but hate commas_ (one subject, so no comma) _We love hyphens, but we hate commas_ (two subjects, so use a comma).

### 16.4.8 COMMA SPLICE

A comma splice occurs when two independent clauses are joined by a comma. If you can put a period where the comma is and both sentences are complete, you have a comma splice: _The dog eats cat food, the cat won't touch dog food_. To fix a comma splice, use a period or semicolon instead of a comma, or add a conjunction after the comma: _The dog eats cat food, but the cat won't touch dog food._

### 16.4.9 MORE COMMA TIPS

- Don't put a comma after _titled_ or _called_ and before a title: _She wrote an essay called "Peace and War."_
- Using a comma to set off _too_ is up to you. If you want emphasis, use a comma.

**PRACTICE EXERCISE 16.4**

## ALL ABOUT COMMAS

Choose the sentence that is properly punctuated.

1.  a.  I have to say, Mary, that you've chosen well.
    b.  I have to say, Mary that you've chosen well.

2.  a.  The oldest man in the group Mr. Sims, is 103.
    b.  The oldest man in the group, Mr. Sims is 103.

3.  a.  The building, which was in the earthquake zone, collapsed.
    b.  The building which was in the earthquake zone, collapsed.
    c.  The building, which was in the earthquake zone collapsed.

4.  a.  Since they left for New York it's been so quiet.
    b.  Since they left for New York, it's been so quiet.

5.  a.  They were going to get a new car, but they decided to book a world cruise instead.
    b.  They were going to get a new car but they decided to book a world cruise instead.

**KEY FOR PRACTICE EXERCISE 16.4**

1.  a
2.  b
3.  a
4.  b
5.  a

# QUIZ FOR CHAPTER 16: PUNCTUATION

For questions 1–20, choose the properly punctuated sentence.

1.  a.  They saw six, old airplanes.
    b.  They saw six old airplanes.

2.  a.  The dog had it's front leg caught securely in the trap.
    b.  The dog had its front leg caught securely in the trap.

3.  a.  Make sure you're ready when we get there.
    b.  Make sure your ready when we get there.

4.  a.  He wants pizza, she wants tacos.
    b.  He wants pizza; she wants tacos.

5.  a.  Leave the premises immediately—or else.
    b.  Leave the premises, immediately or else.

6.  a.  I can't believe, I ate the whole thing.
    b.  I can't believe I ate the whole thing.

7.  a.  We were ready on time, however the plane was delayed.
    b.  We were ready on time; however, the plane was delayed.

8.  a.  John purchased three items on the grocery list: peas, carrots, and licorice.
    b.  John purchased three items on the grocery list: peas; carrots; and licorice.

9.  a.  I liked Kanye West before he got famous.
    b.  I liked Kanye West before, he got famous.

10. a.  Do we really need to go there; or can we stay here?
    b.  Do we really need to go there, or can we stay here?

11. a. He likes to use the saying, "The darkest hour is right before the dawn."
    b. He likes to use the saying; "The darkest hour is right before the dawn."

12. a. Helen Keller once wrote, "Humanity, I am sure, will never be made lazy or indifferent by an excess of happiness."
    b. Helen Keller once wrote, "Humanity, I am sure will never be made lazy or indifferent by an excess of happiness."

13. a. He found a flashlight and carefully entered the dark attic.
    b. He found a flashlight, and carefully entered the dark attic.

14. a. He writes novels, but she writes poetry.
    b. He writes novels but she writes poetry.

15. a. Carol Ann likes her naive sweet roommate best.
    b. Carol Ann likes her naive, sweet roommate best.

16. a. About 1,500 people turned out for an anti-gang-violence walk on Saturday.
    b. About 1,500 people turned out for an anti-gang violence walk on Saturday.

17. a. The calendar app, which you can use on your phone was designed for busy parents.
    b. The calendar app, which you can use on your phone, was designed for busy parents.

18. a. The neighborhood kids all think the big brick house is haunted.
    b. The neighborhood kids all think the big, brick house is haunted.

19.  a.   Our neighbors have an old Ford, and it's just about to fall apart.

     b.   Our neighbors have an old Ford, and its just about to fall apart.

20.  a.   It's time to eat kids.

     b.   It's time to eat, kids.

For questions 21–25, add the proper punctuation to each sentence.

1.   When Brad and Janets car broke down they went to a crumbling ornate mansion for help met some strange people and were never the same again.

2.   Westley joined Fezzik and Inigo to disrupt the princes plans rescue Buttercup kill the count and live happily ever after.

3.   Certification requires a course of study then a practicum working with four and five year olds.

4.   Gerald Halford an infectious disease expert said the outbreak could be easily contained but the vaccine had to be distributed quickly.

5.   The Sanchezes live on the west side their house is next to the Changs.

_____

*Answers can be found on page 203.*

# 17.0

## USAGE AND STYLE TIPS

USAGE AND STYLE

S o much writing advice is out there. The Internet is a wonderful thing, but it's often hard to tell what advice is legitimate and what is someone's personal preference written into a blog post. In this chapter, we'll start by highlighting some of the more common tips and end by busting a few grammar myths.

## 17.1 Word Usage

- *Can* versus *may*: We've probably all at some point asked, "Can I go to the bathroom?" and gotten a snotty "I don't know, *can* you?" response. Yes, traditionally *may* was used for permission and *can* for ability, but for centuries now, *can* has been encroaching into the permission territory formerly occupied solely by *may*. Unless the situation is highly formal (think: court or church), *can* is fine for asking permission.

- *Lay* versus *lie*: This is a tough one, because not only are some of the verb forms the same (*lie/lay/lain* and *lay/laid/laid*), the usage is well on its way to being hopelessly muddled. Who among us hasn't said, "I'm going to go lay down"? Don't sweat this in speech—the grammar police aren't going to knock down your door and carry you off—but realize that in writing you still need to maintain the difference. For now.

  So, how to tell which one you need? If you can swap the verb for a form of *sit* and the sentence still makes sense, you want *lie*: *The dog is <u>lying</u> on the rug / The dog is <u>sitting</u> on the rug*. If you can swap in *put*, use *lay*: *I <u>laid</u> the papers on the table / I <u>put</u> the papers on the table*. It's still tricky, and you may need to look it up every time.

- *Well* versus *good*: James Brown famously sang "I feel good," and, despite what you might have been told, *good* is fine here. When you have a linking verb (see section 6.7), the predicate can be a noun or an adjective. *Good* is an adjective, so it's fine. The next time someone asks "How are you?" you're being perfectly grammatical if you say, "I'm good, thanks."

Of course, "well" can also be an adjective, meaning "not ill," so if you're in good health, you can also use "I am well." Overall, *feel* as a linking verb takes adjectives as complements: *bad* and not *badly*, *happy* and not *happily*, and so on: *I felt bad for them when their dog died. We felt happy at the end of the movie.*

- *Bored of* versus *bored with* versus *bored by*: All three are in use, but *bored of* is the newest and still sounds odd to many people, so it's probably best to avoid *bored of* in professional or formal writing.

- *Go missing*: This synonym for *disappear* came from British English, perhaps through those delightful BBC detective shows. Some people may object, but linguistically it's fine. Use it if you want to.

- *On accident* versus *by accident*: Yes, we do things "on purpose" but they happen "by accident." Unless you're five years old, stick to "by accident."

- *Brung and ain't*: These are common in some dialects of English but should be avoided in formal and professional writing, unless you're writing dialogue or using figures of speech such as "If it ain't broke, don't fix it."

- *Y'all, you guys,* and *guys*: A funny thing happened when plural *you* migrated into the singular spot, displacing *thou* and *thee*—we realized we did indeed need a way to distinguish addressing a group of people from addressing a single person. So we began using new forms to make the plural clear: *y'all* and *you guys* being the most common in US English. Both are common, but because most formal and professional writing won't use the second person anyway, they probably won't come up in writing.

  *Y'all* is common enough that it's almost standard. If you do have occasion to write it, remember that the apostrophe goes between the *y* and the *all*, since that's where the missing letters are.

*You guys* as a form of direct address has largely lost the gendered sense of *guy*—it's common in many parts of the United States to hear women use *you guys* to address a group of female friends—but a third person *guy* as a man is typical outside of direct address: the "cable guy" is a man, never a woman.

## 17.2 When Spell-Check Won't Help

One benefit of technology is that spell-check and autocorrect keep us from making typos or misspelling commonly misspelled words like *separate* and *definitely*. This is a good thing, but where you need to be vigilant in writing is for words spell-check won't catch: the word that isn't the word you want but is still a word.

Homophones—words that sound the same but are spelled differently—are the main culprit here. If you use *affect* when you really mean *effect*, spell-check won't catch it. Here are a few of the most commonly confused homophones:

- *Affect* versus *effect*: I use RAVEN to **R**emember: **A**ffect **V**erb, **E**ffect **N**oun. This isn't 100 percent effective (each can be a noun or a verb in specific situations), but it works most of the time in everyday writing.
- *Peak* versus *peek* versus *pique*: You p**EE**k with your **E**y**E**s. A *peak* is a mountain and a capital **A** looks like a mountain. *Pique* is much less common, but it can be a noun (a fit of pique) or a verb (pique your curiosity).
- *Peddle* versus *pedal*: *Peddle* means to sell, and *pedal* is what you do on your bike. There isn't a nifty trick to remember this one, so if you're not sure, look it up.
- *Palette* versus *palate* versus *pallet*: A *palette* is what a painter uses or is a color scheme. *Palate* is the roof of your mouth or your sense of taste. A *pallet* is a thin mat or one of those wooden platforms cargo is shipped on. There's also no easy trick with this one, so look it up if you need to.
- *Apart* versus *a part*: *Apart* is an adverb or a preposition meaning "separated." *They can never tear us <u>apart</u>*. *A part* is a noun, which means that

if you can drop an adjective between *a* and *part*, you want the two-word version. <u>*A*</u> *(key)* <u>*part*</u> *of the plan is civic responsibility. I would love to be* <u>a</u> *(new)* <u>*part*</u> *of the company.*

- *Rein* versus *reign*: "Rei**G**n" is what kin**G**s do; both have a **G** in them. Reins are for guiding horses, but also have a more figurative sense, like a new leader "taking the reins" or someone having "free rein."

- *Compliment* versus *complement*: Compl**i**ments are n**i**ce things to say—both have an **I**—or n**i**ce things to get when they are compl**i**mentary (free). The two **E**'s in compl**E**m**E**nt compl**E**t**E** each other, just as colors or angles are complementary.

- *Compose* versus *comprise*: A whole "comprises" parts: *The committee* <u>*comprises*</u> *one person from each department.* A whole "is composed of" parts: *The committee* <u>*is composed of*</u> *one person from each department.* Nothing "is comprised of" anything. The easiest way to get this one right is to avoid "comprise" altogether.

## 17.3 Grammar Conventions

**Double negatives**—the most famous probably being the Rolling Stones' "I can't get no satisfaction"—are considered nonstandard, so you should avoid them in writing. The one exception to this is when you have *not* plus a negative adjective, such as *It's* <u>*not uncommon*</u> *for people to do this.*

   **Double genitives**—using *of* plus a possessive, as in *You're a friend* <u>*of mine*</u>—despite sounding redundant, are standard.

## 17.4 Clichés and Wordiness

**Clichés** are phrases that are so common that they've become trite and overused. They are sometimes appropriate, but if you're trying to be fresh and original in your language, it's better to avoid clichés when you can. Common clichés include *at the end of the day, in the wake of, thinking outside the box,* *beating a dead horse, Monday morning quarterback, fight like cats and dogs, not in Kansas anymore*, and so on.

**Wordiness** often occurs when people try to "sound smart" or express themselves overly formally. Most of the time wordiness results in your audience being bored or put off. Clarity never goes out of style, and good speakers and writers help people understand a subject, whatever it may be. Several practices can contribute to wordiness.

- *Smothered verbs* occur when noun + verb is used instead of a verb that means the same thing, as in *made the decision that* instead of *decided* or *conducted an investigation* instead of *investigated*. Smothered verbs aren't wrong grammatically, and sometimes they carry a specific meaning that you need, but be careful not to overuse them.
- *Redundancy* occurs when an idea is repeated unnecessarily, such as *join together* instead of just *join* (which means to bring things together) or *a bright spotlight* instead of just *a spotlight* (spotlights by definition are bright).
- *Sesquipedalianism* means, appropriately enough, "use of long words." Although you shouldn't shy away from a word that is exactly the word you want, even if it's long or uncommon, don't use a big, obscure word when a shorter, clearer one would mean the same thing, unless you are trying to look like a show-off.

## 17.5 Grammar Myths

Over the years, many "rules" have crept into classrooms and usage guides that have no basis in grammar. These grammar myths persist because some people like to cling to what Sister Rosemary told them in eighth grade. You can follow them if you like, but know that they are not real rules of grammar and you can't judge others for not following them. Also, it's probably a better use of your energy to focus on the content and clarity of your writing.

**Myth:** *You can't start a sentence with a conjunction.*
**Fact:** You can. Sometimes the best transition is a simple "but." Don't overdo it, though, because it can get tedious.

**Myth:** *You can't end a sentence with a preposition.*
**Fact:** The sentence "That is the kind of nonsense up with which I will not put" is a classic example of this rule taken too far. Prepositions in English often work as adverbs or pair with verbs, which means they may end a sentence naturally. But even true prepositions don't always have to be followed by their objects. Write however it sounds most natural and is clearest to the reader.

**Myth:** *Don't split infinitives or compound verbs. This means not to put an adverb between the to and the base verb of an infinitive (see chapter 6: Verbs), or between auxiliary verbs and the main verb.*
**Fact:** Split away—there's no basis in English grammar not to put adverbs in the middle; in fact, a sentence often sounds stilted or unnatural when this "rule" is applied.

**Myth:** *You shouldn't use the passive voice.*
**Fact:** Just because a sentence is in the passive voice doesn't mean it's wordy or vague. Sometimes who or what the action is being done to is more important and should start the sentence.

**Myth:** *Since can't mean because.*
**Fact:** *Since* has been documented with the meaning of *because* since the year 1450.

**Myth:** *Cakes are "done," but people are "finished."*
**Fact:** *Done* has been used to mean *finished* for centuries, including with people.  Asking someone "Are you done with that?" is fine.

# QUIZ FOR CHAPTER 17: USAGE AND STYLE TIPS

For questions 1–10, choose the best answer. Use a dictionary if you need to.

1.   All sorts of artists and crafters **peddle / pedal** their wares at the festival.

2.   They were testing to find out the medicine's side **affects / effects**.

3.   It's hard to **peddle / pedal** a bicycle up that hill.

4.   She has a real **flair / flare** for languages.

5.   He wanted to know how the medicine would **affect / effect** him before he drove anywhere.

6.   The school's **principal / principle** is retiring at the end of the year.

7.   The green in that wallpaper really **compliments / complements** the room's rug.

8.   The color **palate / palette / pallet** of the designer's new fall line is warm and bright.

9.   The dogs love to go outside and **lay / lie** in the grass.

10.  **Lay / Lie** those files in my inbox, please.

For questions 11–15, circle the cliché.

11.  Larissa is counting the days until she leaves for Rome.

12.  The speech was full of pie-in-the-sky platitudes.

13.  Even though it was raining cats and dogs, the parade marched as scheduled.

14. He wasn't sick, but he spent all weekend lying on the floor like a beached whale.

15. She studies astrophysics? Well, that's a horse of a different color.

For questions 16–20, match the wordy expression with a similar, more concise one.

| 16. | was chosen as the winner of | regularly |
| 17. | in order to | won |
| 18. | made the statement that | enough |
| 19. | a sufficient number of | said |
| 20. | on a regular basis | to |

For questions 21–25, match the big word with the shorter, clearer one.

| 21. | effectuate | light |
| 22. | substantiate | require |
| 23. | facilitate | confirm |
| 24. | necessitate | achieve |
| 25. | illuminate | ease, help |

*Answers can be found on page 204.*

# GLOSSARY

**abbreviation:** a shorter form of a word or phrase

**acronym:** an abbreviation that uses the first letter of each word in a phrase to spell a pronounceable word

**adjective:** a part of speech that describes a noun, usually answering the question "what kind?" or "which one?"

**adverb:** a part of speech that describes a verb, adjective, or other adverb, usually answering the question "where?" "when," "how?" or "why?"

**agreement:** the grammatical concept that nouns and pronouns and subjects and verbs have to match each other in number

**aspect:** a verb quality indicating whether an action is complete or ongoing

**auxiliary verb:** a form of *be*, *have*, or *do* that combines with other verb forms to indicate tense, aspect, and mood

**clause:** a group of words that has both a subject and a predicate

**conjugation:** the process by which verbs change to indicate tense, person, number, and aspect

**conjunction:** a part of speech that joins words, phrases, or clauses in a sentence

**determiner:** a word that goes with a noun or noun phrase to shape its meaning

**direct object:** a noun or pronoun that follows an action verb and indicates what was done

**gerund:** a verbal form that works like a noun

**homophone:** a word that is pronounced the same as another word but spelled differently

**imperative:** a verb mood that expresses a command

**indicative:** a verb mood that states a fact, asks a question, or expresses an opinion

**indirect object:** a noun or pronoun that indicates the recipient of a direct object

**infinitive:** the unconjugated *to* form of a verb

**initialism:** an abbreviation that uses the first letter of each word in a phrase

**interjection:** a part of speech that indicates a strong emotional outburst

**intransitive verb:** a verb that does not have a direct object

**linking verb:** a "being" verb rather than a "doing" verb

**modal:** a kind of auxiliary verb that indicates something's possible, allowed, suggested, or necessary

**noun:** a part of speech that indicates people, places, things, ideas, or concepts

**number:** whether a noun, pronoun, or verb is singular or plural

**participle:** a verbal form that works like an adjective

**phrase:** a group of words that work as a unit of meaning and may have a subject or predicate but not both

**portmanteau:** a word formed by combining two words into one

**possessive:** a noun, pronoun, or adjective that indicates belonging to or association with

**predicate:** what comes after the subject to finish the sentence: the verb, usually plus a direct object or subject complement

**preposition:** a part of speech used to tie nouns to other information in the sentence

**pronoun:** a part of speech that stands in for a noun or noun phrase

**subject:** a noun or pronoun that does, or is, the verb

**subject complement:** a noun or adjective that comes after a linking verb and tells more about the subject

**subjunctive:** a verb mood used for hypothetical and contrary-to-fact situations

**tense:** a verb quality indicating whether an action happened in the past, present, or future

**transitive verb:** a verb that has a direct object

**verb:** a part of speech that indicates an action or a state of being

# FURTHER READING

Grammar advice is everywhere, but sometimes it's hard to know what's reliable or at the level you're looking for. Here are some resources for further exploration:

**Detailed style and usage manuals:**

*Garner's Modern English Usage* (fourth edition, 2016) by Bryan A. Garner: Every serious writer needs this.

*The Chicago Guide to Grammar, Usage, and Punctuation* (2016) by Bryan A. Garner

*Merriam-Webster's Dictionary of English Usage* (1994)

**Classic style and usage manuals (that is, some advice may be dated but interesting from a historical perspective, and much of the information is still valid):**

*The Careful Writer* (1965) and *Dos, Don'ts, and Maybes of English Usage* (1977) by Theodore M. Bernstein

*Words on Words* (1980) by John B. Bremner: Bremner's ornery sense of humor makes even the outdated entries a pleasure to read.

*The Elements of Style* (fourth edition, 1999) by William Strunk and E. B. White: This little guide has taken a lot of criticism recently, not because it's full of bad advice, but because people take it as gospel instead of guidelines. Start with it; don't end with it.

**Writers' guides:**

*On Writing Well* (sixth edition, 1998) by William Zinsser: A classic.

*Help! for Writers* (2011) by Roy Peter Clark: Steps for getting ideas and putting drafts together.

*The Sense of Style* (2014) by Steven Pinker: A guide for making academic and professional writing more engaging.

**Books about language and grammar that aren't strictly manuals:**

*Miss Thistlebottom's Hobgoblins: The Careful Writer's Guide to the Taboos, Bugbears, and Outmoded Rules of English Usage* (1971) by Theodore M. Bernstein: A classic; but largely good advice even today.

*Lapsing into a Comma* (2000), *The Elephants of Style* (2004), and *Yes, I Could Care Less: How to Be an English Snob Without Being a Jerk* (2013) by Bill Walsh: Walsh's engaging writing, interesting facts, and practical advice make these books a delight for anyone interested in usage, grammar, and writing.

*The Transitive Vampire* (1984) and other grammar books by Karen Elizabeth Gordon: Fun examples and clear explanations make these books a good way to romp through some of the finer points of grammar.

**Online advice:**

Purdue OWL (Online Writing Lab): owl.english.purdue.edu/owl/: Comprehensive, clear, and reliable.

Common Errors in English Usage: public.wsu.edu/~brians/errors/errors. html: A huge list of words and phrases that are commonly confused and misused, and explanations of how to use them correctly.

# QUIZ ANSWER KEYS

## KEY FOR CHAPTER 3 QUIZ

1. blue / adjective
2. the / determiner
3. Yikes! / interjection
4. bus / noun
5. perform / verb
6. quickly / adverb
7. but / conjunction
8. in / preposition
9. we / pronoun
10. freedom / noun
11. scientists, Alaska, data
12. returned, calculated
13. climatic
14. once
15. from
16. you
17. can't go, is
18. too
19. hey
20. the, the

## KEY FOR CHAPTER 4 QUIZ

1. it's
2. you're
3. should've
4. didn't
5. effects (RAVEN: Remember: Affect Verb, Effect Noun)
6. caliber (preferred US spelling)
7. peek (you pEEK with your EyEs—two E's each)
8. rein (reiGn is what a kinG does—both have a G)
9. scarier

10. puddling
11. ratted
12. armies
13. its (no apostrophe—it doesn't mean *it is*)
14. kittens
15. PBS's
16. your
17. midnight
18. November 19, 1911, (don't forget the second comma!)
19. $3,000
20. 10,000
21. December
22. your p's and q's
23. First
24. '60s

## KEY FOR CHAPTER 5 QUIZ

1. subject
2. relative clause
3. complement
4. prepositional phrase
5. direct object
6. b
7. b
8. c
9. a
10. c
11. independent
12. dependent
13. independent
14. dependent
15. independent
16. d
17. c
18. e
19. a
20. b
21. misplaced modifier (Did the whole staff just get discharged from the hospital?)
22. nonparallel construction (The last element is not a noun phrase.)
23. misplaced modifier (Who or what is facing a severe budget shortfall?)
24. no error
25. nonparallel construction (The middle element is missing a verb.)

## KEY FOR CHAPTER 6 QUIZ

| | | | |
|---|---|---|---|
| 1. | a | 14. | a |
| 2. | b | 15. | a |
| 3. | a | 16. | a |
| 4. | b | 17. | d |
| 5. | c | 18. | c |
| 6. | b | 19. | b |
| 7. | d | 20. | d |
| 8. | b | 21. | think |
| 9. | a | 22. | thought |
| 10. | c | 23. | had; finished |
| 11. | b | 24. | were |
| 12. | a | 25. | were growing |
| 13. | b | | |

## KEY FOR CHAPTER 7 QUIZ

1. Some / quantifier
2. The / article
3. That / demonstrative
4. Which / interrogative
5. Her / possessive

# KEY FOR CHAPTER 8 QUIZ

| Noun | Plural | Possessive | Possessive plural | Common or proper? | Count or noncount? |
|---|---|---|---|---|---|
| 1. star | stars | star's | stars' | common | count |
| 2. McLain | McLains | McLain's | McLains' | proper | count |
| 3. audience | audiences | audience's | audiences' | common | count (collective) |
| 4. pity | n/a | pity's | n/a | common | noncount |
| 5. octopus | octopuses | octopus's | octopuses' | common | count |
| 6. runner | runners | runner's | runners' | common | count |
| 7. Super Bowl | Super Bowls | Super Bowl's | Super Bowls' | proper | count |
| 8. Joanna | n/a | Joanna's | n/a | proper | count |
| 9. hot dog | hot dog | hot dog's | hot dogs' | common | count |
| 10. obesity | n/a | obesity's | n/a | common | noncount |

## KEY FOR CHAPTER 9 QUIZ

1. initialism (*NGO*, short for *nongovernmental organization*)

2. acronym (*scuba*, short for *self-contained underwater breathing apparatus*)

3. initialism (*CEO*, short for *chief executive officer*)

4. portmanteau (*brunch*, short for *breakfast + lunch*)

5. clipped form (*etc.*, short for *et cetera*)

6. initialism (*MBA*, short for *master of business administration*)

7. portmanteau (*staycation*, short for *stay* [home] + *vacation*)

8. clipped form (*rec*, short for *recreation*)

9. initialism (*AD*, short for *anno Domini*)

10. acronym (*USA PATRIOT*, short for *Uniting and Strengthening America by Providing Appropriate Tools Required to Intercept and Obstruct Terrorism*)

11. acronym (*PAC*, short for *political action committee*)

12. clipped form (*rom-com*, short for *romantic comedies*)

13. portmanteau (*docudrama*, short for *documentary + drama*)

14. clipped form (*lit*, short for *literature*)

15. acronym (*UNESCO*, short for *United Nations Educational, Scientific and Cultural Organization*)

## KEY FOR CHAPTER 10 QUIZ

1. Whose
2. its; its
3. I
4. they
5. me
6. who
7. whom
8. who
9. me
10. their
11. Does
12. its
13. live

14. Who
15. your
16. me
17. was
18. I
19. personal
20. reflexive
21. interrogative and relative
22. demonstrative and relative
23. indefinite
24. interrogative
25. possessive

## KEY FOR CHAPTER 11 QUIZ

1. 7 French
2. 3 little
3. 5 triangular
4. 1 two
5. 8 silk
6. 4 old
7. 6 green
8. 2 gorgeous
9. fastest
10. younger

11. farther (or further)
12. smartest
13. more important
14. most peaceful
15. better
16. compound
17. comparative
18. proper
19. indefinite
20. superlative

## KEY FOR CHAPTER 12 QUIZ

1. passionately / manner
2. furiously / manner
3. well / degree
4. yesterday / time
5. extremely / degree
6. Apparently / sentence
7. Nevertheless / conjunctive
8. now / time
9. moreover / conjunctive
10. out / location

## KEY FOR CHAPTER 13 QUIZ

1. out / adverb (where)
2. on / adjective (which one)
3. from / adjective (which one)
4. from / adverb (why)
5. at / adverb (where)
6. about / adjective (what kind)
7. after / adverb (when)
8. on / adverb (where)
9. before / adverb (when)
10. with / adjective (which one)

## KEY FOR CHAPTER 14 QUIZ

1. whenever / subordinating
2. and / coordinating
3. both . . . and / correlative
4. or / coordinating
5. not only . . . but also / correlative
6. even though / subordinating
7. wherever / subordinating
8. neither . . . nor / correlative
9. but / coordinating
10. so / coordinating

## KEY FOR CHAPTER 15 QUIZ

1. Wow
2. Yikes
3. Whoa
4. Oh, no
5. blam

6. Awesome
7. Holy cow
8. Wait
9. yay
10. yuck

## KEY FOR CHAPTER 16 QUIZ

1. b
2. b
3. a
4. b
5. a
6. b
7. b
8. a
9. a
10. b
11. a
12. a
13. a
14. a
15. b
16. a
17. b
18. a
19. a
20. b
21. When Brad and Janet's car broke down, they went to a crumbling, ornate mansion for help, met some strange people, and were never the same again.
22. Westley joined Fezzik and Inigo to disrupt the prince's plans, rescue Buttercup, kill the count, and live happily ever after.
23. Certification requires a course of study, then a practicum working with four- and five-year-olds.
24. Gerald Halford, an infectious-disease expert, said the outbreak could be easily contained, but the vaccine had to be distributed quickly.
25. The Sanchezes live on the west side; their house is next to the Changs'.

## KEY FOR CHAPTER 17 QUIZ

1. peddle
2. effects
3. pedal
4. flair
5. affect
6. principal
7. complements
8. palette
9. lie
10. lay
11. counting the days
12. pie-in-the-sky
13. raining cats and dogs
14. like a beached whale
15. a horse of a different color
16. won
17. to
18. said
19. enough
20. regularly
21. achieve
22. confirm
23. ease, help
24. require
25. light

# PRACTICE EXERCISES AND QUIZZES

# INDEX

# ABOUT THE AUTHOR

**Lisa McLendon** runs the Bremner Editing Center at the University of Kansas journalism school, where she also teaches editing, writing, and grammar. She was formerly a copy editor at the *Wichita Eagle* and launched her journalism career on the copy desk at the *Denton Record-Chronicle* after earning a Ph.D. in Slavic linguistics from the University of Texas. She lives in Lawrence, Kansas. Follow her on Twitter @MadamGrammar.